California DESERTS

Jerry Schad

FALCON™

Helena, Montana

FRONT COVER PHOTO
Glorieta Canyon in Anza-
Borrego Desert State Park
by Larry Ulrich.

BACK COVER PHOTOS
Desert stream by
Jerry Schad (top left),
moth in desert aster by
Jerry Schad (bottom left),
and chuckwalla by
Larry Burton (right).

"Cabbage tree" was one of the many names given the Joshua tree by early travelers. The tough, resilient branches of this tree at Queen Valley in Joshua Tree National Park seem to reach for the firmament. LARRY ULRICH

Library of Congress Number: 87-082470
ISBN: 1-56044-546-7

Design, typesetting, and other prepress work by Falcon Press, Helena, Montana. Printed in Hong Kong.

*This book is dedicated to you, the reader, in the hope
that you will come to find the same peace and grandeur
I have found in California's deserts.*

"It is stern, harsh, and at first repellent. But what tongue shall tell the majesty of it, the eternal strength of it,
the poetry of its wide-spread chaos, the sublimity of its lonely desolation! And who shall paint the splendor
of its light; and from the rising up of the sun to the going down of the moon over the iron mountains,
the glory of its wondrous coloring?" —John C. Van Dyke, *The Desert* LARRY ULRICH

"The region . . . is, of course, altogether valueless. After entering it there is nothing to do but leave. Ours had been the first, and will doubtless be the last, party of whites to visit this profitless locality."—Lieutenant Joseph C. Ives, U.S. Topographical Engineers, in a report on an early reconnaissance of the desert. KEITH D. LAZELLE

Contents

Below the granitic crags of Joshua Tree's Coxcomb Mountains, nature lays out a welcoming carpet of dune primrose and sand verbena. DAVID MUENCH

California deserts

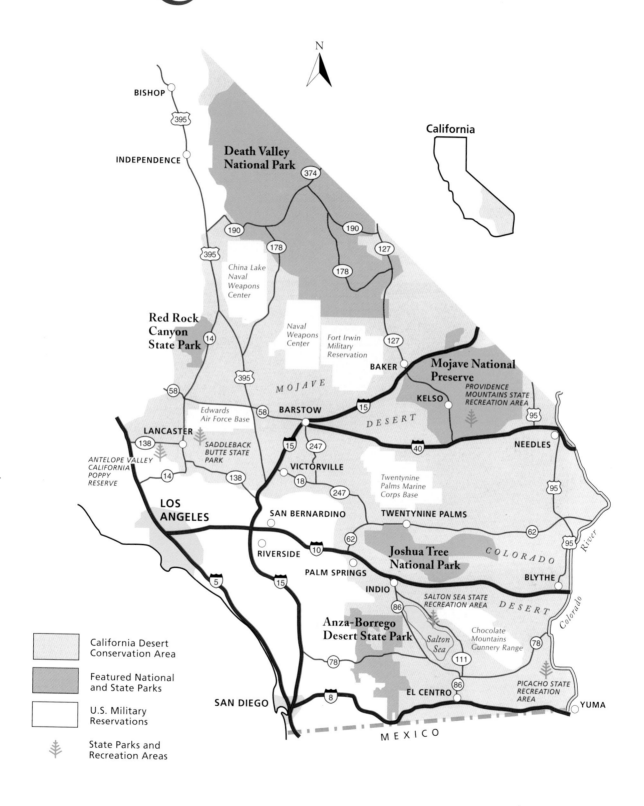

California

BISHOP

395

INDEPENDENCE

N

Death Valley National Park

374

190

190

178

127

178

China Lake Naval Weapons Center

Red Rock Canyon State Park

14

395

Naval Weapons Center

Fort Irwin Military Reservation

127

BAKER

Mojave National Preserve

PROVIDENCE MOUNTAINS STATE RECREATION AREA

58

KELSO

95

Edwards Air Force Base

58

MOJAVE

DESERT

BARSTOW

15

40

NEEDLES

LANCASTER

138

SADDLEBACK BUTTE STATE PARK

15

247

VICTORVILLE

95

ANTELOPE VALLEY CALIFORNIA POPPY RESERVE

14

138

18

247

Twentynine Palms Marine Corps Base

COLORADO

LOS ANGELES

SAN BERNARDINO

TWENTYNINE PALMS

62

95

RIVERSIDE

62

10

PALM SPRINGS

Joshua Tree National Park

BLYTHE

5

15

INDIO

86

SALTON SEA STATE RECREATION AREA

DESERT

Colorado River

Anza-Borrego Desert State Park

Salton Sea

Chocolate Mountains Gunnery Range

78

78

111

PICACHO STATE RECREATION AREA

California Desert Conservation Area

Featured National and State Parks

U.S. Military Reservations

State Parks and Recreation Areas

SAN DIEGO

8

EL CENTRO

86

YUMA

MEXICO

(RIGHT) Magenta-hued flowers of a hedgehog cactus hide the plant's long spines. KAZ HAGIWARA

(BELOW) Watered by a cold cataract, these native plams in the Santa Rosa Mountains outside Palm Springs drink freely at their roots while their crowns bask in the sun. The hardy brittlebush, on the other hand, meets the desert head on. With the approach of summer, the daisy-like flowers drop, and its leaves shrivel and curl in response to drought and heat.
DAVID MUENCH

California's leanest quarter

A cactus spine stabs the ankle. A warm breeze cools sweat-soaked clothing. Desiccated air catches in the throat. A brutal, unrelenting sun shimmers out of the blue glare of the midday sky. Water glints along polished rock. A canyon wren trills dolefully from somewhere in a shady canyon wall. Creosote bushes reek under receding thunderheads. The inexpressible perfume of desert lavender wafts on the night air.

These sensations and others, some deliriously pleasurable, some distinctly annoying, some mysterious, await you on your first—or one hundredth—trip into the California Desert. But you will never come to know them unless you explore. You must walk—or at the very least roll down the car windows, turn off the air conditioner, and let the warm desert air wash over you.

First-time explorers beware: the desert doesn't coddle. It is harsh and uncompromising to the unprepared. Yet it does give quarter to patient and inquiring minds. Learn to accept its moods, discover its secrets, and partake of its unique treasures.

One of its unique treasures is something so obvious it might go completely unrecognized at first: the incomparable openness and spaciousness of the desert landscape. Distances are deceiving here. Through the transparent desert air, your

Kit fox tracks lead toward an alkali deposit at Mesquite Flats in Death Valley National Park. KAZ HAGIWARA

Dainty, gentle, and alert in appearance as well as behavior, the kit fox prowls the open, sandy desert or arid grasslands where its prey—small rodents, lizards, and insects—abound. STEPHEN J. KRASEMANN/DRK PHOTO

gaze can easily stretch across hundreds of thousands of acres of empty plains backed by denim-blue summits maybe fifty or a hundred miles away. Beyond even that, the seamless sky, larger than life, vaults over the horizon.

Covering about 25 million acres—roughly the entire southeastern quarter of California—the California Desert rivals the state of Virginia in area. Stretching 375 miles north to south and 275 miles east to west across its midsection, it boasts of immense, unpopulated areas perfectly suited to all kinds of recreation, some of the most productive agricultural areas in the nation, important mineral and energy resources, a number of huge military installations, and a modest but rapidly growing population.

Another unobvious treasure is the silence, the unaccustomed absence of sound found nowhere else in nature except perhaps in snowbound mountains during a lull in a storm. On barren sand dunes, in the lifeless clay hills of the badlands, and in water-

less canyons cut deep into the flanks of the driest mountain ranges, you may hear no sound but that of the wind. Without that, the silence is profound. The slightest movement, or breath, or even the sound of one's own heartbeat, breaks the spell.

The California Desert conceals a stunning variety of plants and animals. Here and there across the foothills and arroyos, thin trickles of water arise from rock and sand to nourish mini-oases of wild grape vines, willows, and cottonwoods. In secluded, boulder-strewn canyons palms hold aloft crowns of shimmering green fronds. Coyotes sing on the flats, and bighorn sheep survey their domain from atop the crags. At night the desert yields to creatures that seldom venture forth by day.

Some of the most wicked forms of cactus thrive in the California Desert, but so do mosses, ferns, sedges, and many other types of water-loving vegetation. Here are plants that perish without a permanent supply of water, and plants that die a hundred little deaths, only to be revived time and again by the slightest moisture. Here are stony soils that lie almost inert under the sun for a decade or more, then burst forth with a multi-hued carpet of wildflowers after the right combination of rainfall and sunshine. Here are rodents that live a lifetime without drinking a drop of water and fish that thrive in shallow saline pools reaching temperatures of more than 100 degrees.

Although most people know a desert when they see one, any precise definition of a desert is subject to opinion. A climatologist, for example, might define a desert in terms of rainfall and temperature. An average of, say, ten inches or less of precipitation annually and hot summers make a desert. A geographer might take into account such factors as soil types and evaporation potential. A botanist, on

(RIGHT) Teddy-bear cholla spines frame a cactus wren's view of the world. "The vegetable kingdom has not produced anything else so fearfully armed," wrote one expert on California cacti in reference to the cholla. D. CAVAGNARO

the other hand, might recognize a desert by the kinds of plants growing within it.

In general, experts draw a distinction between "true" deserts and marginal ones—arid, treeless, grass-covered lands called "steppes." With rainfall of ten to fifteen inches per year, parts of the southern Central Valley, the Los Angeles Basin, and other areas in central and southern California once fit the description of steppes very well. Today, of course, they've been transformed by water brought from afar by aqueducts. The swaying palm trees and exotic landscaping of coastal southern California and the rich farmlands of the San Joaquin Valley are only a thin veneer of lushness over what is basically near-desert.

East of the mountains, however, there's no doubt. The California Desert receives about two to five inches of rainfall in an average year, with some areas consistently receiving two inches or less. Even so, the California Desert is less arid than most of the other deserts in the world. The interior of the Sahara receives barely one inch of rain per year, and South America's Atacama collects less than half an inch a year.

The California Desert is but a small outlying wedge of the great North American Desert, which extends over much of the American Southwest. The North American Desert is, in turn, only one of twelve major arid regions throughout the world.

Because the North American Desert displays such a remarkable diversity of vegetation patterns and geographical features, many attempts have been made to divide it into separately classified units. One popular view pictures five divisions—the Great Basin, Mojave (also spelled "Mohave"), Sonoran, Painted, and Chihuahuan deserts. All these divi-

California's state flower—the California poppy—blankets these hillsides above the Antelope Valley, beginning about March. The floral display is limited to just four to six weeks. By summer these hills will be brown and sere. CARR CLIFTON

sions have somewhat inexact boundaries because of overlapping vegetation and geographic patterns.

California claims parts of the Mojave and Sonoran deserts, plus (arguably) narrow slivers of the Great Basin Desert that intrude into California along the Nevada border both north and south of Lake Tahoe. This book, however, does not cover these Great Basin slivers, which more properly belong to Nevada and parts of Oregon, Idaho, and Utah.

Because of its great range of elevation, climate, and flora, the Mojave has been called the most varied and interesting of all the North American deserts—a suggestion that might raise the hackles of a Sonoran Desert-loving Arizonan. A little over half the Mojave Desert lies in California with the remainder in southern Nevada.

California's share of the huge Sonoran Desert, which extends east across Arizona and deep into northwestern Mexico, is a relatively small one. Because that share is bounded on the east by the Colorado River, it long ago acquired the name "Colorado Desert."

From a topographical point of view, the Mojave Desert is a "high" desert because of its relatively higher elevations (and resulting cooler temperatures), and the Colorado Desert is a "low" desert. Of course, there's an exception to every rule—Death Valley, located comfortable within the Mojave Desert, is actually the lowest piece of real estate around.

Except where the two deserts—Mojave and Colorado—border each other, vegetation provides a way to distinguish them. An important indicator

Salt deposits in this mineral spring add color to the desert landscape. D. CAVAGNARO/DRK PHOTO

plant of the Mojave Desert is the Joshua tree. This tree-sized yucca grows only at middle to upper elevations, as does its smaller cousin, the Mojave yucca. Low-lying basins in the Mojave Desert often are dominated by uniform-looking stands of creosote bush, bur sage, and other small desert shrubs.

The Colorado Desert vegetation is more diverse than that of the Mojave. Creosote bush and bur sage cover the flats here, too, but along the arroyos and washes are distinctive growths of taller plants: mesquite, palo verde, ironwood, and smoke tree. Rocky slopes are dotted with ocotillo, brittlebush, and more kinds of cactus than area usually found in the Mojave. A well-known symbol of the Colorado Desert is the California fan palm, flourishing where permanent water is present.

In both the Colorado and Mojave deserts sparse "forests" of juniper and pinyon pine maintain a tenuous existence on the slopes and crests of the higher mountains. These pocket habitats may not conform to the strict definition of desert, but they are still considered a part of it.

California deserts may look lean and hungry, but they are most assuredly not wastelands. They are endowed with subtle physical beauty, remarkable plants and animals, and an indescribable ambience that neither words nor photographs can fully capture. Read on and discover more. ▓

Day by day, capricious winds sculpt an everchanging Death Valley sand dune. Turbulent air flowing immediately above the surface of the sand produces fingerprint-like ripples. DAVID MUENCH

Yesterday and today

The earliest Californians left behind an archaeological treasure trove of reminders—stone and bone tools, projectile points, basket fragments, pottery fragments, rock rings and cairns, fish traps, roasting pits, burial mounds, grinding stones and bedrock mortars, petroglyphs (rock etchings), pictographs (rock paintings), and intaglios (huge patterns of human or animal forms made by removing stones from the flat desert floor). About fourteen thousand separate prehistoric sites have been identified in the California Desert so far. Tens of thousands more lie in wait for future discovery.

The date of the earliest human occupation of the California Desert area is not only unknown, it is a figure subject to intense controversy. Radioactive dating of the Yuha Man—skeletal remains found under a cairn in the Yuha Desert (near El Centro in the southwestern Colorado Desert)—indicates an age of at least 21,500 years. But dates of more than 200,000 years are claimed for tools apparently fashioned by humans at the Calico Early Man Site north of Barstow. Another estimate, based on rock flakes excavated along with the tooth of a mammoth at China Lake in the Mojave Desert, gives a date of 42,000 years before the present. Some of these estimates are wildly at odds with recent evidence that the earliest wave of human emigration into the Americas (across an ice-free land bridge

At Giant Figures National Historic Landmark near Blythe, ancient art competes with the modern doodles of off-road vehicles. Fences around both figures now protect them from vandalism. CRAIG AURNESS/WEST LIGHT

from Asia to Alaska) took place only about 30,000 years ago.

Controversies aside, it's quite certain that by ten thousand years ago, rather large numbers of aboriginal peoples had ranged over present-day California. This was at the close of the Pleistocene epoch (1.6 million to 10,000 years ago), when ice-age glaciers were receding in the Sierra Nevada and a milder, wetter climate prevailed throughout today's desert area. Streams and lakes were fringed with marshes supporting a variety of wildlife and edible plants. Today's dry lakes and basins (such as the floor of Death Valley) were brimming with glacial meltwater hundreds of feet deep. Humans hunted (with spears and darts, not bows and arrows), fished, and gathered easily obtained plants.

As the climate became hotter and drier during the ensuing millennia, a more nomadic, plant- and seed-gathering culture displaced the earlier one. Technological improvements included baskets and grinding tools. Hunting continued, but the ripening of plant foods controlled the movements of a band. Still later, technology was further advanced by contact with more advanced cultures to the east. Use of the bow and arrow became widespread by about two thousand years ago, and pottery was introduced by about one thousand years ago.

The migration patterns followed by many of the recent California Desert Indians were dictated by

(RIGHT) Remembrances of an unfathomable culture, these petroglyphs, decorating the basaltic walls of Renegade Canyon in China Lake Naval Weapons Center, may be three thousand years old. FRED HIRSCHMANN

(FAR RIGHT) Thrust upward by capillary action along the shore of a drying lake some two thousand years ago, the rock-hard salt pinnacles of Devils Golf Course in Death Valley National Park are kept razor sharp by occasional cloudbursts. DAVID MUENCH

the seasons. During the cooler part of the year, mesquite beans, agave hearts, yucca flowers, palm and cactus fruits, grasses, greens, buds, and dozens of other kinds of vegetable food were gathered or harvested from lower elevations in the desert. Pinyon nuts and (wherever available) acorns were collected from the nearby mountains in summer and fall. "Ollas" (earthen pots) were used to store seeds and nuts and to transport water.

Jackrabbits were harvested during communal hunting drives, and other small game animals were dispatched by throwing stick or bow and arrow.

Stained-glass irridescence highlights the pleated surface of a dying California fan palm frond. The dead fronds droop to form a thick skirt around the trunk, providing a habitat for rodents, lizards, and snakes. D. CAVAGNARO

Along the lower Colorado River and the shore of the prehistoric Lake Cahuilla (the predecessor of the Salton Sea), enterprising Indians caught fish in rock-lined traps or snagged them with hooks fashioned from cactus spines. They also practiced agriculture to a limited extent, pushing the seeds of maize, beans, squash, and gourds into flood-dampened soils.

Of the roughly 300,000 Indians living in California before the coming of the Spanish, relatively few occupied the deserts. Food resources were simply too scarce. The desert Indians belonged to only two of California's twenty or so major language groups. They were the Shoshonean group of the Mojave and northern Colorado deserts and the Yuman group of the southern Colorado Desert and lower Colorado River area. These language groups were further subdivided into language subgroups, or nations—the Mono, Koso, southern Piute, Serrano, Cahuilla, Kamia, Yuma, Chemehuevi, and Mohave—each of which occupied a fairly large, exclusive territory. The desert Indian nations, in turn, consisted of close-knit extended-family units, independent of one another except for intermarriage and trade. Respect for the rights of others and peace usually prevailed.

The era of Spanish exploration began in a small way at first. In 1540 (two years before Juan Rodriguez Cabrillo's celebrated visit at San Diego Bay and thirty-nine years before Francis Drake's landing near Point Reyes on the northern California coast) two Spanish expeditions, one from the south commanded by Hernando de Alarcon, and the other from the east commanded by Melchor Diaz, reached the lower Colorado River in the vicinity of Yuma, Arizona. Members of both expeditions, many historians believe, set foot on the west bank of the river north of Yuma, so becoming the first non-Indians to step inside the boundaries of present-day California.

European explorers continued to move along the Pacific coast, but more than a century and a half elapsed before white men again would visit the California Desert. In the years 1701 and 1702, the

Spanish missionary Father Eusebio Kino traveled west from Sonora, Mexico, and southern Arizona to proselytize in the lower Colorado River region. His reconnaissance of the area provided convinc-

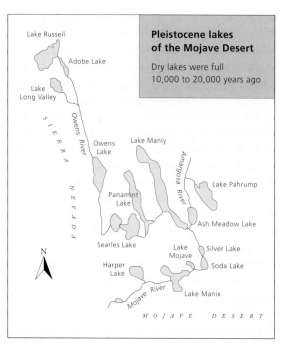

Pleistocene lakes of the Mojave Desert

Dry lakes were full 10,000 to 20,000 years ago

Bedrock mortars are found at Indian sites throughout California. These, in the upper reaches of Borrego Palm Canyon, were used to mill acorns. The resulting meal was leached to remove the tannin, then boiled as gruel or baked into acorn bread. JERRY SCHAD

ing evidence that, contrary to long-held notions, California was not an island. Again after a long interval, in the 1770s, Pedro Fages, Juan Bautista de Anza, and Francisco Garcés blazed a variety of routes across both the Mojave and Colorado deserts. Anza opened an important new land route across the Colorado Desert linking Spanish outposts in Sonora with settlements on the California coast.

Starting in 1820, American trappers—so-called "mountain men" like Jedediah Smith, James Pattie, Ewing Young, and Joseph Walker—intruded into Spanish- and later Mexican-governed California territory, ostensibly to try their luck at trapping. Some were thrown into prison and later released with stern commands to leave California at once. Several may have been spying on behalf of the American government. By the 1840s, many of these same mountain men were busy escorting wagon trains full of emigrants and even an invading army across the desert trails to the fertile coastal valleys. The Mexicans were defeated by the Americans in 1847, and California became first a territory, then a state of the Union.

With the opening of the American period and the Gold Rush of 1849, tens of thousands of emigrants streamed into California by land and sea. One of the most popular land routes from the Midwest—the all-weather Southern Emigrant Trail—funneled travelers through the Colorado Desert, while another led across the Mojave Desert. The Indian population, meanwhile, was declining disastrously, partly as a result of armed conflict and forced relo-

"Pile it high," said the boss, and Chinese laborers fell to the task. These borax "haystacks" west of the Harmony Borax Works date from just after the turn of the century, when the mining company was required to show developmental work on patented land. RICK MCINTYRE/DVNM

The Anza expeditions

By the end of 1769, the Spanish explorer Gaspar de Portola and Father Junipero Serra had worked their way well up the California coast establishing missions and presidios (forts). An important task remained—the establishment of a direct land route between these outposts and the older Spanish settlements of Sonora, Mexico. This route would lead across the unknown Colorado Desert and over the mountains separating the desert from the coastal foothills and valleys of today's southern California.

On January 9, 1774, a small party of soldiers and adven-turers led by Juan Bautista de Anza set out to fulfill this challenge. Leaving the pueblo of Tubac, Sonora (near present-day Tucson, Arizona), they headed west across the barren wastes toward the Colorado River. Before crossing the river, the party chanced upon an Indian who had recently traveled the route they were seeking. The Indian was immediately drafted into service as a guide.

After crossing the Colorado, the party became hopelessly lost wandering in dune sand (today's Imperial Dunes) and was forced to retreat to a water hole to recuperate for several weeks. By March, a remnant of the expedition pressed onward, this time successfully outflanking the dunes by looping well to the south. Turning north and crossing the present-day international border, they came upon a good well and evidence of a trail which the Indian guide recognized.

With success practically assured now, the party continued north, reaching a point not far from the southwestern shore of the present Salton Sea. They then turned northwest into Borrego Valley and up Coyote Canyon to a conspicuous pass at its head. Beyond this lay a series of coastal valleys leading directly to the San Gabriel Mission near Los Angeles. Anza and his men arrived on March 22.

On returning to Sonora, Anza was commissioned to lead a second expedition into California, this time with a large contingent of colonists, soldiers, and livestock needed to populate the coastal pueblos and ranchos as far north as San Francisco. While crossing the Colorado Desert west of today's Imperial Valley in December 1775, members of this expedition had to endure extreme cold, high winds, and snow—highly unusual weather conditions then as now. After losing much of its livestock, but no human lives, the expedition

proceeded onward to the San Gabriel Mission and eventually Monterey and San Francisco.

Despite the recognition given to Juan Bautista de Anza as originator of the first emigrant trail across the California Desert, there was an earlier expedition over part of the same route. In 1772 Pedro Fages, the Spanish military commander of California, led a detachment of three soldiers east from San Diego in search of army deserters who reportedly had fled inland. Fages traveled into the present-day Anza-Borrego Desert, then turned northwest along the route through Coyote Canyon, later rediscovered by the Anza expeditions. The Fages party proceeded over Cajon Pass, traversed a corner of the Mojave Desert, dropped down into the San Joaquin Valley, and finally reached San Luis Obispo near the coast.

Unlike the Fages expedition, which was hastily conceived and executed, Anza's expeditions were extraordinarily well documented. The detailed records and diaries kept by Anza and other members of his party have kept open an important window to the past—a window that allows us a frank glimpse into the lives of the hardy Spanish settlers and explorers, as well as the lives and cultures of the desert-dwelling Indian tribes they encountered along the way. ■

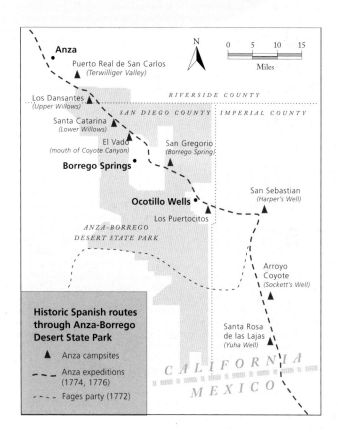

Historic Spanish routes through Anza-Borrego Desert State Park

▲ Anza campsites

- - - Anza expeditions (1774, 1776)

-·-·- Fages party (1772)

cation but also because of introduced diseases and alcohol.

While most travelers of the nineteenth century thought of the California Desert as nothing better than a wasteland to be crossed as quickly as possible, a few visionaries took a less jaundiced point of view. As early as the mid-1800s there was talk of irrigating the below-sea-level areas of the Colorado Desert (today's Salton Sea and Imperial and Coachella valleys) by shipping water through canals from the Colorado River. One promoter nearly succeeded in persuading the state and federal government to grant him a whopping ten million acres—nearly all of today's Imperial and Riverside counties—in exchange for supplying irrigation water.

As yields diminished from the goldfields of the Mother Lode, hard-rock miners began turning east toward the Mojave Desert and Death Valley. Early explorations led to a big strike in 1865 with the discovery of large deposits of silver and lead at Cerro

The Salton Sink and the Flood of 1905-07

In the youthful heyday of the reclaimed Imperial Valley, few of the new settlers had time or energy to worry about one disturbing aspect of their agricultural paradise—the irrigation canal they depended on drew water from a river nearly four hundred feet higher than the below-sea-level fields they tilled. No one anticipated that, as a consequence of human folly and natural forces, the mighty Colorado River, forty miles away, would jump its banks, wander through Mexico for a distance, and then turn north to fill the dry Salton Sink as it had many times in the geological past.

Starting in early 1905, a series of floods breached the intake of the canal. By August nearly the entire flow of the Colorado was captured by the canal and began filling the Salton Sink. Attempts to return the river to its original channel with sandbags and brush mats were futile.

During the next summer's seasonal floods, the whole of the Colorado River flow filled a new Salton Sea, raising its level seven inches a day over an area of four hundred square miles. A thousand-foot-wide waterfall developed near the shoreline, cutting back through the soft alluvial deposits of the valley at a pace of nearly a mile a day. Homes and farms disappeared in its wake. A corner of Calexico and nearly half of Mexicali were sliced away by a chasm fifty feet deep.

The Southern Pacific Railroad Company finally came to the rescue. Engineers laid out a spur line to the intake site, built temporary bridges across the flooding channels, then moved in flat cars and dump cars by the thousands, filled with loads of rock and gravel. Hundreds of workers toiled day and night pitching the rock overboard by hand. After repeated failures, success came at last: the Colorado River was back in its channel by February 1907.

Today, a permanently altered landscape bears mute testimony to one of nature's strangest rampages. On both sides of the border, the cutback chasms are still missing a volume of dirt nearly four times as great as that excavated from the Panama Canal. And the Salton Sea survives—larger yet than Lake Tahoe. ■

(LEFT) While the tiny resort community of Salton Sea Beach slumbers, a twenty-mile stretch of open water mirrors the dawn. The Salton Sea, created by accident in 1905-07, occupies the largest below-sea-level basin in the Americas. JERRY SCHAD

Gordo in the Inyo Mountains. Soon all sorts of rabble were combing the desert for riches, incited by sensational newspaper reports and fanciful rumors. One rumor had it that somewhere in the desert was an Indian tribe using golden bullets for ammunition. During the next half century of booms and busts, much ore was pulled out of the dry mountain ranges and valleys east of the Sierra Nevada. But transportation and processing costs were proportionally as high. Few hard-rock mining operations actually turned a profit.

Borax mining, on the other hand, became a more successful and sustained commercial enterprise. By the 1870s, large deposits of this little-known mineral used mostly in pharmaceutical products had been discovered at several sites in California and Nevada. As new applications for borax—in soaps and detergents, cosmetics, and porcelain glazes—were realized, a boom materialized. Twenty-mule teams hauling immense wagons full of refined borax lumbered across Death Valley for several years until richer and more conveniently located deposits were discovered elsewhere in the Mojave. The borax mystique, of course, was perpetuated well into the twentieth century through movies and the radio and television series "Death Valley Days." Today there are at least a dozen major industrial uses for borax and borate products.

By the late 1880s parts of the California Desert were becoming domesticated, if not civilized. Industrialists harvested Joshua trees for the production of paper pulp—a scheme that failed but not before destroying thousand of acres of Joshua-tree woodland. Settlers ran cattle over the desert grasslands and attempted to dry farm on marginal soils. Patients with tuberculosis and other respiratory illnesses were discovering the therapeutic value of clean, dry air. A railroad through Barstow and Needles was completed in 1883 by the Southern Pacific—only the first of several that would crisscross both the Mojave and Colorado deserts by the early 1900s. Easy access to formerly remote areas opened up the possibility of settlement and tour-

ism. Small communities arose along the tracks to serve railroad workers and travelers. The first desert resort hotel was established at Palm Springs in 1886.

This first wave of civilization was accompanied by instances of wild land speculation. Speculators divided the western Mojave—on paper at least—into thousands of town lots, and the gullible snapped them up at boom prices. In one celebrated instance, a clever promoter judiciously trimmed the Joshua trees in and around his proposed subdivision on the desert outside Los Angeles, then spiked the bayonet-like leaves of each tree with cheap, windfall oranges. He then shipped in a throng of wealthy Eastern tenderfeet, serving them plenty of beer, wine, and whiskey. The Easterners stood agape as the area was described as "the only spot west of the Rocky Mountains where the orange is indigenous." With proper irrigation, they were told, the trees would bear oranges the size of pumpkins. The promoter's bluff and bluster paid off. Many lots were sold, but no houses were ever built.

Soon after the turn of the century, earlier visions of large-scale desert reclamation became reality. A canal from the Colorado River transformed what an early Spanish explorer had called "the Land of the Dead" into the Imperial Valley, a salad bowl for the nation. The march of progress, though, was not without dissent. Famed naturalist and writer John C. Van Dyke, a forerunner of today's environmentalists, wrote in 1901: "The deserts should never be reclaimed. They are the breathing-spaces of the West and should be preserved forever." Reclamation did continue, of course, with parts of the Coachella, Palo Verde, and Antelope valleys coming under plow in the ensuing decades.

In 1913 the city of Los Angeles, anticipating its future water needs, completed the first of two aqueducts spanning the western reaches of the Mojave Desert from the Owens Valley to the San Fernando Valley. Roads began to extend across the desert after World War I, and highway settlements sprang up to serve the ever-increasing numbers of automobile travelers. The Colorado River was impounded at Parker Dam, and a huge aqueduct, constructed between it and Los Angeles, gave the Southland a taste of water collected from the Rocky Mountains. A new All-American canal into the Imperial Valley replaced the former one crossing Mexican soil. Long-distance power lines from Boulder Dam appeared, interrupting the flat, empty vistas of the Mojave.

Inspired by articles in popular magazines such as *Out West*, *Sunset*, and *Touring Topics*, tourists from southern California's burgeoning cities were enticed to visit the desert and discover for themselves the value of wide-open, unspoiled landscapes. Sentiment

evolved for the creation of parks and preserves. In 1922, Congress passed a bill that would have created a Palms National Monument near Palm Springs, but it was never implemented because Indians who owned most of the land in question vetoed the idea. In 1933, however, conservationists

(BELOW) The copious consumption of water, along with the use of air conditioning, has made the Palm Springs region a year-round playground for wealthy retirees and visitors alike. The area boasts forty-two golf courses and more than fifteen thousand swimming pools.
JAMES RANDKLEY

were successful in establishing both the huge Death Valley National Monument and Borrego Palms Desert State Park—the predecessor of today's sprawling Anza-Borrego Desert State Park. A third big slice of park land, Joshua Tree National Monument, was set aside in 1936.

With the coming of World War II, military concerns eclipsed all else in the desert. Preparing for North African warfare, General Patton's tanks lumbered across vast stretches of the California deserts. The Army Air Corps and the Navy appropriated immense tracts of federal land for the training of recruits and the testing of aircraft and weapons.

Today, the rumble of distant guns, the shriek of jet aircraft, and the sparkle of flares ignited during nighttime maneuvers are familiar to desert visitors.

About three million acres of the California Desert remain permanently locked up in the form of military reservations: the sprawling Marine Corps Training Center at Twentynine Palms, the largest marine base under the U.S. flag; the army's Fort Irwin National Training Center, a proving ground for tanks as well as soldiers; the Naval Weapons Center at China Lake, where Sidewinder missile and other advanced weapons are developed and tested; and Edwards Air Force Base, where an immense natural landing field—the sixty-five-square-mile Rogers Dry Lake—and superb aviation weather have brought out the right stuff in fliers from Chuck Yeager to space-shuttle astronauts to the pilots of the latest experimental flight vehicles. Smaller military holdings within the California Desert include supply depots, pilot training facilities, and areas set aside as bombing ranges.

Heavy military use of some areas has rendered them virtually worthless for any other future purpose. The long-inactive Carrizo Impact Area, for example, now technically a part of Anza-Borrego Desert State Park, remains closed indefinitely to all visitors despite several attempts to clear it of unexploded ordnance. The China Lake Weapons Center, on the other hand, is carefully managed to protect its rich archaeological resources, which in-

Umbilical cord to both the Imperial and Coachella valleys, the All-American Canal slips under Interstate 8. Completed in 1940, the canal slices through the same sand hills that thwarted Juan Bautista de Anza's first push across the California Desert in 1774.
CRAIG AURNESS/WEST LIGHT

With a ready supply of water, almost anything is possible on the desert. This reclaimed parcel lies near Blythe.
CRAIG AURNESS/WEST LIGHT

clude some of the most elaborate petroglyph displays found anywhere in the West.

Civilian industrial and population growth paralleled the influx of the military, especially after World War II. Modern boomtowns mushroomed around Edwards and the other military installations of the western Mojave. Businesses and industries started up or relocated there to take advantage of cheap land and military-related spinoffs. And many military retirees stayed on in the area.

With pick-and-shovel mining methods a distant memory, large corporations took over the business of mineral extraction. Relatively few sites were deemed valuable enough for large-scale operations,

and thousands of other prospects were abandoned. Today, immense volumes of mineral-bearing earth are quarried and processed at places like Boron in the western Mojave, where an open pit now yawns 475 feet deep, three quarters of a mile long, and half a mile wide. The daily output of borates from this mine alone is greater than all the borax taken out of

(RIGHT) Its receptive radio ear turned ever skyward, the Goldstone Deep Space Tracking Station in the Mojave Desert remains an essential communication link between far-ranging planetary space probes and controllers at the Jet Propulsion Laboratory in Pasadena. CRAIG AURNESS/WEST LIGHT

Screaming in from earth orbit, America's space shuttles reach landfall on the flat hardpan surface of Rogers Dry Lake at Edwards Air Force Base. CRAIG AURNESS/WEST LIGHT

Death Valley during its twenty-mule-team heyday. Gypsum, chloride salts, and strategic minerals like molybdenum, tungsten, and rare earths, not to mention gold, also play an important role in mining the desert.

By mid-century a renewed land boom hit. Residents of the burgeoning coastal cities began to think of the desert not only as an interesting place to visit but also as an inexpensive, uncrowded place to live. From the late thirties to the sixties, the Bureau of Land Management (BLM) deeded or sold many hundreds of thousands of acres of surplus federal land, mostly on the western and southern fringes of the Mojave Desert. "Jackrabbit homesteaders" by the thousands built twenty-foot-square shacks on five-acre lots as vacation or retirement homes. Many of the new homesites were on land not only desolate but totally removed from any easily obtained source of water as well.

While some of these homestead developments evolved into respectable communities over the years, many today show the marks of neglect and vandalism. Palm Springs, on the other hand, was destined from the beginning to become an exclusive resort and retirement community colonized by celebrities from Hollywood. Today, Palm Springs and its sister cities down along the Coachella Valley have become a true metropolis—California's gilded answer to Phoenix and Tucson.

The sixties and seventies saw a veritable explo-

Spinning out the kilowatts, wind turbines by the thousands dot the desolate northern reaches of the Coachella Valley just below San Gorgonio Pass. The strong, steady winds out of the pass also attract board sailors, here practicing their sport on a percolation pond used to replenish groundwater for urban and agricultural uses. CRAIG AURNESS/WEST LIGHT

sion in the use of off-road vehicles in the California Desert. Easy access into many formerly remote areas became possible, greatly increasing the demand on the desert's scenic but fragile resources. The lack of management on many public lands outside the parks and national monuments resulted in irresponsible and damaging uses.

In the late seventies the development and testing of new technologies created practical uses for the desert's boundless resources of sun and wind. The experimental Solar One power plant near Barstow was constructed, and wind turbines were erected along breezy passes. Paralleling the explosion of communications technologies, microwave relay stations popped up along desert ridges.

In response to conflicting pressures on federal lands throughout the nation, Congress in 1976 passed a landmark bill, the Federal Land Policy and Management Act (FLPMA), to manage all public lands and create the California Desert Conservation Area (CDCA)—a special administrative boundary drawn around California's 25 million acres of desert. In 1980, the BLM, custodian of

about half of the conservation area at the time, completed a comprehensive management plan seeking a balance between purely utilitarian uses such as mining, grazing, and energy production, and other uses such as recreation and wildlife protection. More than 80 separate areas of unspoiled character were nominated for wilderness status within the BLM's domain.

By the mid-1980s a movement was afoot to enact a law that would elevate the status of Death Valley and Joshua Tree national monuments to national

A swirl of vehicle lights surrounds campers in the Imperial Sand Dunes east of the Imperial valley. On busy weekends, as many as forty thousand off-road vehicle enthusiasts rendezvous here.

CRAIG AURNESS/WEST LIGHT

parks, to create a new national park in the eastern Mojave Desert, and to protect as wilderness nearly all of the candidate wilderness areas identified by the BLM. After nearly a decade of controversy and political maneuvering, President Clinton signed the California Desert Protection Act into law in October 1994. In accordance with this act, both Death Valley and Joshua Tree national monuments were expanded in size by about one-third (to 3.3 million acres and 1.0 million acres respectively) and designated national parks. The former East Mojave National Scenic Area, managed by the BLM before the signing of the desert protection act, became the 1.4-million-acre Mojave National Preserve. (National "preserves" differ from national parks and monuments in that certain uses, such as hunting, grazing, mining, oil drilling, and off-road driving may be permitted in the preserves. In the Mojave preserve, hunting and trapping are authorized; oth-

erwise, the preserve is managed as a national park.)

The California Desert Protection Act also created 69 separate wilderness areas—more than 7.6 million acres worth—spread throughout the California Desert Conservation Area. These new desert wilderness areas join other areas previously declared as wilderness within the desert national parks. The term "wilderness," when applied to public lands, means lands essentially untouched by human-caused changes, offering outstanding opportunities for primitive and unconfined forms of recreation, having valuable natural features of some kind, and generally greater than 5000 acres in size. Designated wilderness areas are protected from environmental degradation by prohibitions on vehicle travel and commercial exploitation.

Some twenty million people now reside in the southern half of California (primarily within 50 miles of the ocean), while less than a million people

Arrayed to track the sun's diurnal course across the sky, Solar One's 1,818 heliostats reflect sunbeams to a central receiving tower where water is boiled to generate electricity. MARK E. GIBSON

live in the desert itself. "Nowhere else in the world," states a BLM report, "is so much easily accessible public land so close to a large, restless, highly mobile metropolitan population." The California Desert Protection Act should ensure that California's southeastern quarter remains the biggest reservoir of open space in the state.

Nonetheless, pressure for increased development of the desert's resources will surely continue, as will demands for recreational uses. The shy, desert-dwelling bighorn sheep and other solitude-loving creatures may be forced to retreat still farther from the sights and sounds of civilization. These and other challenges, some unimaginable today, await the desert of tomorrow. ▣

Desert enthusiasts enjoy a wide variety of recreation at Dumont Dunes. CRAIG AURNESS/WEST LIGHT

California's bare bones

Geologists love deserts. With little vegetation to screen the earth's naked surface, deserts bear (and bare) the marks of both recent changes and ancient upheavals dating back hundreds of millions of years.

Until the development of the theory of plate tectonics, geologists could only scratch their heads and speak in terms of "unknown forces" when trying to explain the desert's—indeed all of California's—baffling geologic record. Today a coherent overview, if not the exact details, of the origin and movements of the desert's various rock formations is coming into sharper focus.

The entire western margin of North America is largely an amalgamation of many separate, smaller masses that were rafted to and docked against a continental core over a period of about 200 million years. Amazingly, many of these bits and pieces added to North America have come thousands of miles from points west and south. This migration was accomplished by the landforms riding "piggyback" atop

A sharply folded anticline in the sandstone wall of Split Mountain at Anza-Borrego Desert State Park shows the effects of unimaginable pressures deep within the earth. Free of obscuring vegetation and sliced cleanly by flash floods, exposed rock such as this frequently speaks volumes about its geological history. BILL EVARTS

large and small drifting pieces of crust—or plates—which, taken altogether, form the earth's solid but fractured skin. (To put these grand-scale tectonic movements in perspective, we should note that most plod along at about the growth rate of a fingernail.)

Tens of millions of years ago in the vicinity of present-day California, the big North American Plate (on which most of North America rides to-

Rock fragments embedded in the wall of Death Valley's Mosaic Canyon were transported to this site millions of years ago, buried by alluvium, reassembled deep underground by heat and pressure to form a metamorphic rock called breccia, and finally exposed again by erosion. JAMES RANDKLEV

day) was colliding with and overriding a drifting oceanic plate to the west. The leading edge of this oceanic plate was subducted, or forced downward, under the North American Plate and melted by the earth's interior heat. Less dense than its surroundings, the accumulating molten material (magma) began to rise. Some of it reached the surface, touching off volcanic eruptions. The rest slowly cooled and solidified while still at a depth of several miles. (Subduction continues today in the Pacific Northwest, where Mount St. Helens and other Cascade Range volcanoes vent pent-up energy from the melting of a small plate being subducted under a part of western North America.)

While subduction was forming volcanic mountain ranges in California, the material on top of the overridden oceanic plate—sea floor, whole volcanic islands, and even chunks torn from other continents to the west or south—was scraped off and plastered onto the western edge of the North American Plate. Some of these bits and pieces of crust including blocks of limestone, beds of metamorphosed sea-bottom ooze, and the cores of ocean-born volcanoes, are now exposed in the bedrock of the California Desert.

But more than just old volcanic deposits and flotsam and jetsam make up today's desert formations. The material that solidified deep underground during the era of subduction played an important role, too. This material evolved into huge plume-shaped masses of granitic rock called plutons. The plutons rose toward the surface and displaced older deposits, which were eroding away. Long chains of plutons, called batholiths, now form the backbones of both the Sierra Nevada and the Peninsular ranges—the two great northwest-southeast-trending ranges that define the western edge of the desert. These batholiths continue to rise today, building up the mountain crests just a little faster than erosion wears them down.

Farther inland, in the Mojave Desert, isolated plutons have bobbed to the surface to create a number of smallish mountain ranges. So distinctive is this kind of rock that four totally separate ranges in the western and central Mojave were unimaginatively labeled the "Granite Mountains."

Another of subduction's aftereffects molded the "Basin and Range" province, which extends east of the Sierra Nevada as far as the Rocky Mountains. Here the North American Plate seems to be overriding a partially digested remnant of an oceanic plate that was swallowed about thirty million years ago. Movements between the two cause the crust above to lift and stretch and fracture into mostly parallel blocks. Some blocks, forced upward, form elongated mountain ranges like those that flank Death Valley; others are sinking like the floor of Death Valley itself.

Because of the stretching, the continental crust east of the Sierra Nevada is now among the thinnest and weakest anywhere in the world. This has permitted volcanic activity to continue into the present era. As a result, fresh cinder cones and volcanic flows dot the landscape east of the Sierra Nevada, north and south of Death Valley, and in the central Mojave Desert.

About twenty-five to thirty million years ago, the huge Pacific Plate, once located far to the west, came close enough to touch the North American Plate. The two plates started sliding sideways against each other along a broad front of the western North American continent (a motion that continues today). A sliver of mainland Mexico, which had overridden the Pacific Plate, broke away and floated northwest at a rate of about two inches per year, relative to the rest of North America. Ten million years ago, this sliver was asserting its independence as a detached finger of land—the Baja California peninsula—newly separated from the mainland by the forming Gulf of California.

Today the northern part of the sliver makes up the wedge of California lying west of the boundary between plates—the great rift known as the San Andreas Fault. It continues to ride northwestward on the Pacific Plate, but not always smoothly. Because of friction between the moving plates, tension builds up over the years that when suddenly released, causes California's most devastating earthquakes.

Striking southeast across the edge of the Mojave Desert near Palmdale, the San Andreas Fault slips through Cajon Pass, enters the Colorado Desert north of Palm Springs, then slides inconspicuously along the eastern shore of the Salton Sea, where it disappears in the deep sediments of the below-sea-level Salton Trough. (The Salton Trough is simply a structural extension of the Gulf of California—part of the rift left behind when the Baja peninsula tore away from mainland Mexico. Were it not for a berm of silt deposited at the head of the gulf by the Colorado River, the gulf would extend northward to lap at the shores of Palm Springs suburbs.) Many geologists believe the next massive earthquake in California—likely to occur within fifty years—will be triggered by a sudden release of tension along this section of the fault.

But California is not split by just one rift. Thousands of faults have been mapped in the deserts alone. Some are splinter faults of the northwest-southeast-trending San Andreas, while others are detached, north-south trending faults. Movements along these faults occur in every conceivable direction: horizontally, vertically, and obliquely. One major fault—the Garlock Fault—takes off from a bend in the San Andreas to run northeast-southwest across the Mojave Desert. Movements along both the Garlock and San Andreas faults are exerting a vise-like force on a big block of the western Mojave, rotating and squeezing it eastward. The east-west-trending Transverse ranges, which form the southern boundary of the Mojave Desert, also seem to have been affected by rotation.

Faults have contributed not only to the desert's intricate geomorphology but to the movement of groundwater as well. Subsurface water moving under pressure is often pushed upward along cracks or planes of weakness within the fault zones, producing springs, both hot and cold. Here, water-loving plants can establish a firm foothold. On the edge of the Coachella Valley, for example, seepage of groundwater along the San Andreas Fault has produced a line of palm oases stretching for more than thirty miles.

While it's clear that grand-scale movements associated with plate tectonics have roughed out the general design of the California Desert, it's difficult to get a feel for these processes on a human scale. Even nongeologists, though, have no trouble both seeing and understanding the more immediate and spectacular effects of erosion.

Erosion polishes and buffs, and rips and tears. Like a high-strung artist, the forces of erosion may ignore or half-heartedly pick away at a desert landform for years, then in a brief burst of inspiration, create a natural work of art. And, like the proverbial frustrated artist, erosion can destroy in minutes a masterpiece a thousand years in the making.

Erosion is driven by the actions of both wind and water. Since desert areas are dry and windy with plenty of sand and dust, wind erosion is expected and understandable. Not so the flow of water. A classic irony of the California Desert is that even with meager amounts of rainfall, water is the sharpest and most effective tool of erosion. There are three reasons for this: first, rocks and unvegetated soils in the desert shed water quickly; second, steep slopes are common, so runoff is rapid; and third, rainfall, although minimal on average, occasionally comes in short-lived but intense summer thunderstorms.

During these cloudbursts, rivulets of water cascading down gullies on every slope join together to form rushing torrents—flash floods—that churn their way down the lower canyons. Rocks and sand particles suspended in the rushing water scour the bottoms and sides of these gullies and canyons—in effect tearing down the slopes particle by particle and rock by rock.

As the debris-laden flood water rushes out of the confines of a canyon and spreads out below the canyon mouth, boulders and heavier gravel settle out first. Smaller stones and particles wash farther downslope. In time, after many episodes of flooding, a convex, fan-shaped accumulation of debris called an alluvial fan develops. Boulders lie where they were dropped at the fan's apex, while the finer particles, carried farther on a slackening flow, collect at the fan's base.

Where several alluvial fans from adjacent canyons along a mountain range overlap, a broad, gently sloping sheet called a "bajada" (from the Spanish word meaning "lower slope") forms. In a real sense, desert mountains are simultaneously being leveled by erosion and buried by the slow buildup of debris in the fans and bajadas around them. Only mountain ranges experiencing uplift are able to keep head and shoulders above their own debris.

Stand on the surface of an alluvial fan or bajada, and you might easily imagine the infrequent but steady geological creep of its contents. Pick up a handful of rocks or sand and know that these once were a part of the mountain above you; earlier, perhaps, they belonged to an ancient volcano, a molten mass of underground granite, or maybe a hardened chunk of sea floor which could have originated thousands of miles away.

Beyond even the lower edges of alluvial fans and bajadas, the smallest particles of sand and silt are carried still farther by flood waters. Everywhere in California's deserts, except along a narrow strip next to the Colorado River, that alluvium ultimately ends up in the bottoms of the down-dropped basins, or sinks, that lie among the mountain ranges. When the flood waters finally evaporate, a layer of clay particles remains to form a firm, flat surface called a playa, or dry lake. If the water has come from a considerable distance, it may contain dissolved salts, especially those of sodium and calcium, which then are precipitated out on the playa to form a salt pan.

Usually water need travel only a short distance to reach a sink. A curious exception is the Mojave River—a true desert river in the sense that it arises along the desert's edge on the northern slope of the

Flood-gouged channels, some old, others relatively new, score the surface of a classically formed alluvial fan above Saline Valley in the northern Mojave Desert. BARBARA BRUNDEGE/EUGENE FISHER

Lonely survivors in a sea of sand, creosote bushes anchor a small hillock amid the dunes on Death Valley's floor.
RENE PAULI

San Bernardino Mountains and flows across more than a hundred miles of the Mojave Desert. Early explorers discovered this to be a river that, quite the opposite of normal rivers, dies away as it flows downhill. Evaporation and percolation into porous soils steal its vitality before it reaches its endpoint—the Mojave River Sink.

The Colorado River, on the other hand, is a desert interloper. Since most of its flow comes from tributaries draining the Rocky Mountains and the high plateaus of Arizona and Utah, it is regarded as an "exotic" river with respect to the desert. In much the same way, the Nile River is exotic with respect to the northern Egyptian desert.

Aside from tearing down mountain ranges, water erosion has fashioned the most intricately sculpted territory in the California Desert—the badlands. Here soft sedimentary deposits from geologically recent times—sandstone, siltstone, mudstone, and clay—are too weak to resist the violent rains. Depending upon the particular types of deposits present, the running water cuts near-vertical, accordion-pleated receding cliffs; chisels narrow, steepwalled "slot canyons"; carves broad, sinuous channels flanked by razor-backed ridges; or simply rounds off all sharp corners in dried mud or clay deposits, creating sensuous-looking, totally barren hills. Weaknesses in certain kinds of formations give rise to arches, natural bridges, and winding mud caves. These fanciful, sometimes haunting patterns and constructions are found around Zabriskie Point in Death Valley, in Rainbow Basin north of Barstow, at Red Rock Canyon State Park in the western Mojave, in the Mecca Hills east of Palm Springs, and in the Borrego and Carrizo badlands of Anza-Borrego Desert State Park.

The lack of water and typically alkaline soil in the badlands dictate a hard life for those few plants and animals that can survive here. Often, however, these same areas are a rich repository of the fossil-ized remnants of former life. Since the badland sediments were originally deposited as silt and mud on sea floors and freshwater marshes alike, a wide variety of fossils, both marine (corals, shellfish) and nonmarine (petrified wood, fossilized bones), are present.

The other agent of erosion—wind—is less important on the grand scale but often locally significant. Winds strong enough to pick up dust particles may carry them aloft for hundreds of miles. On very windy days the crystalline air and blue sky over Death Valley and the other big desert basins may be

The shapes of sand dunes

Barchan dunes form where sand is scarce and the wind comes from one direction. Barchans stand apart from each other, each having a crescent shape with tapered tails pointing downwind. A steep "slip face" forms on the inner (concave) edge where sand grains blown over the top of the dune come to rest.

Star dunes form when a limited amount of sand is trapped in an area where the wind blows equally from several directions. In a sense, these are modified barchans.

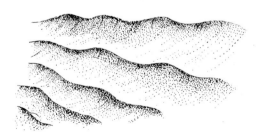

Transverse dunes are the result of moderate one-directional winds acting on a large quantity of sand. Wind eddies create a series of parallel ridges perpendicular (transverse) to the prevailing wind direction.

Longitudinal dunes, or seif (sword) dunes, occur when strong prevailing winds act on a large amount of sand. They may result from the coalescence of many barchan dunes. Longitudinal dunes are characterized by deep-cut troughs parallel to the direction of the winds.

sacrificed to a depressing whitish or brownish haze extending upward thousands of feet.

Strong winds also pick up sand particles—tough, hard grains like quartz that have weathered from the surfaces of larger rocks. Seldom, however, can the wind lift these heavier particles more than two or three feet above the ground. That's no comfort, of course, if you are stuck in the open desert on foot, or driving along a notorious stretch of Interstate 10 east of Palm Springs during the worst of the early spring windstorms. As surely as a blast of sand stings the legs, frosts automobile paint and glass, and weakens utility poles, it sculpts the contour of all natural objects in its path.

Like the sweepings of the world, sand collects wherever the winds care to deposit it. Sand particles blown by prevailing winds over the top of a low ridge or mountain will drop out on the lee side, accumulating to form a cottony blanket of "blow sand." Larger accumulations in the open desert make up dunes, some anchored in place by vegetation or a particular combination of opposing winds, others marching across the desert floor at a constant creep as particles are catapulted over a dune crest and fall to form a "slip face."

Compared with the Arabian and other deserts of the Old World, the California Desert is relatively sand-poor: less than five percent is covered by dunes. Yet some of these dune fields are spectacular. The Algodones Dunes (also known as the Imperial Dunes or Sand Hills) stretch like a luminous veil for forty miles south and east of the Salton Sea. The Eureka Dunes northwest of Death Valley and the Kelso Dunes east of Barstow reach heights of nearly seven hundred feet, enough to rival the tallest dunes in the world.

Despite its sometimes static and timeless appearance, the California Desert is geologically restless, both above and below its surface. As we will see in following chapters, the desert is equally dynamic in its climate and biology. ▩

A land of extremes

Palm Springs bakes under a furnace-like sun and 110-degree-plus air temperatures, while just over the mountains and across the coastal plain, thermometers register 70 degrees under an overcast sky. One side of a coastal mountain range sports forests of oak and pine, while the other drops barren and sheer to the brown floor of the desert. Such ironies aren't uncommon in California.

Southern California lies in a subtropical latitude where high pressure and cloudless skies prevail. This is because global air circulation patterns deliver most of the moisture in the atmosphere to the tropical and temperate belts, including regions well north of California's deserts, sparing little for areas in between.

Much of the moisture that does reach California originates in swirling storms that spin out of the North Pacific below Alaska. These migrate southeastward toward the North American coastline, following "storm tracks" that shift with the seasons. In summer, these storms normally reach land north of California, sprinkling the northern part of the state but seldom affecting the southern half. In

Winter's gloom settles upon the upper elevations of Joshua Tree National Park. Joshua trees require well-drained soils, moderate precipitation, and occasional spells of subfreezing weather—conditions ideally satisfied at elevations of about 4,000 feet throughout most of the Mojave Desert. DAVID MUENCH

winter, however, the storms pack a bigger punch and tend to sweep farther south, often drenching the state from Oregon to Mexico.

California's mountain ranges provide the explanation for the added dryness of the interior desert. As moisture-laden clouds from Pacific storms move onshore, they rise to cross the mountain barriers. While rising, they cool, and the moisture condenses into precipitation over the windward slopes and crests of the mountains. In the lee (east or southeast) of the mountains, the inland-moving air descends and warms. The remaining water vapor tends not to condense further. California's deserts, then, lie in the "rain shadow" of the mountains.

During the advance of a weak storm, rain clouds usually evaporate before reaching the desert. They billow tantalizingly over the western mountains but deliver nothing to the desert below. More powerful winter Pacific storms, though, sometimes push over the mountain barriers to give the desert a long, gentle soak.

The Coast ranges and the Sierra Nevada screen the northern Mojave Desert, while the Transverse ranges, which lie south of the Sierra Nevada, screen parts of the southern Mojave. Since most of the Mojave lies at moderate elevations, it catches more moisture than lower-elevation deserts. (But don't bother with your umbrella in Death Valley. Its low

elevation and position behind not one, but several shadowing mountain ranges make it one of the driest spots on the continent.) The generally lower, hotter, and drier Colorado Desert is screened by the Peninsular and Transverse ranges.

Both deserts, but especially the Colorado, get some rainfall from tropical air masses that often intrude into eastern California during the late summer. Originating as far away as the Gulf of Mexico and the southeastern Pacific Ocean, these storms, in the form of enormous cumulus clouds reminiscent of Armageddon, pile up against the desert ranges and release brief, violent downpours. In recent decades, "chubascos"—tropical summer storms moving north from the Gulf of California—have wreaked havoc around Palm Springs and in the Anza-Borrego area.

Rainfall rates measured at most weather stations in the California Desert typically range from two to five inches per year. Death Valley's average is a paltry 1.63 inches—less than the rate for any other station in the United States, but not lower than the rates measured near the head of the Gulf of California just south of the Mexican border.

The rainfall records confirm a meteorological axiom: the less the average precipitation, the greater the variation from year to year. At Yuma, Arizona, just across the Colorado River from the southeastern tip of California, yearly precipitation has ranged from a meager 0.28 inch to a respectable 11.42 inches. And at Bagdad, a lonely railroad stop in the southern Mojave Desert, no rain fell at all during one spell of 767 days, though the annual average there is over two inches.

Besides stealing moisture that might otherwise green the parched desert landscape, the mountains

Summer flood waters, laden with suspended silt, sand, gravel, and sometimes boulders, churn down a small wash and slide across Highway 78 in Anza-Borrego Desert State Park. Drivers should exercise caution and avoid such floods if at all possible. Attempting to cross a dip such as this could prove extremely unwise.
PAUL R. JOHNSON

Badwater Basin: Lowest, hottest, and driest place in the United States

Amid the thousands of acres of glaring, lifeless salt pan in Death Valley's Badwater Basin are two distinct spots the U.S. Geological Survey recognizes as having the lowest elevation in the western hemisphere—minus 282 feet. At midday in the summer, human existence is either extremely uncomfortable or impossible here. The sun's radiation, reflected and concentrated by the salt surface, slowly roasts exposed skin. Low humidity sucks moisture from the pores at a truly alarming rate.

There's no sign of human intervention out here on the salt pan, only the mindless yet orderly mechanics of physics and chemistry. A repetitive polygonal pattern of rock-salt ridges, enclosing salt flats a few feet across, spreads in all directions. This pattern is created when shallow floodwaters evaporate. The salt precipitates out of solution within and above underlying mud cracks.

Flanking Badwater Basin on both the east and west are the Amargosa and Panamint ranges, which act together to confine sun-warmed masses of air. Sometimes even the nighttime temperature fails to drop below 100 degrees. The Panamints, which rise to an elevation of more than two miles, cast a rain shadow over the basin as well.

Badwater Basin is fifteen miles south of (and slightly lower than) the nearest weather station, at Furnace Creek, where the highest official air temperature in the western hemisphere has been recorded—134 degrees. But Furnace Creek lies in a minibelt of tempered climate, where surface water and vegetation tend to reduce the temperature and increase the humidity. Temperatures at the Badwater pools, on the edge of Badwater Basin, have historically averaged about four degrees higher than at Furnace Creek, though records for that site are not complete.

Having already won kudos as the western hemisphere's lowest place and as the driest place in the United States, Badwater Basin might deserve recognition as the hottest place on earth as well. ∎

In the calm of a January morning, this inches-deep pool of saline water at Badwater Basin holds an image of the Panamint Range. The snow-dusted summit to the left of center is 11,049-foot Telescope Peak. TOM ALGIRE

forming California's spine tend to isolate the interior deserts from the moderating influence of the marine air from the west. Rarely do the cool fog banks that creep inland into the San Joaquin Valley or the coastal plains of southern California sneak over even the lowest passes to reach the desert. This isolation from the ocean, coupled with uninterrupted sunshine most days, promotes high daytime temperatures in the desert. This is especially true in June and July, when the sun stays above the horizon for up to fourteen hours.

On an average day, the ground surface and lower atmosphere of the desert absorb about ninety percent of the solar radiation; only ten percent is deflected back into space by dust particles or clouds. Along the coast, on the other hand, the ground surface soaks up only about half of the sun's heat; the rest is absorbed by clouds of water vapor, thicker plant cover, and the ocean.

The efficient transfer of heat in the desert works the other way, too. Desert temperatures plummet at night as ninety percent of the day's accumulated heat radiates through the clear, dry atmosphere into space. Along the coast, the humid and often cloudy atmosphere overhead acts as an insulating blanket, keeping the thermometer at a moderate register. Experienced desert campers always bring with them plenty of warm clothing and bedding: they know desert temperatures can seesaw by as much as 50 degrees.

Cut off from the moderating influence of the Pacific Ocean and unprotected from the extreme "continental" climate of interior North America (across which masses of both frigid polar air and warm tropical air freely move), the deserts also experience extreme seasonal variations in temperature. In the higher Mojave, winter brings cool days and dependably subfreezing nights, while in summer the daytime temperature normally tops 95 degrees for weeks at a time. At Borrego Springs (elevation 600 feet), only fifty-five miles by crow's flight from the San Diego County coastline, record high and low temperatures are 121 degrees and 15 degrees—typical of many Colorado Desert locations.

Of prime interest statistically, of course, is the highest temperature ever recorded in the California Desert. Death Valley is the undisputed champion, with a 134-degree reading on July 10, 1913. This was the world's record until 1922, when a high of 136.4 degrees was measured at El Azizia in the Libyan Sahara. These temperatures are measured in the shade five feet above the ground. Under the blazing midday summer sun, the ground gets much hotter. In fact, a ground temperature of 201 degrees has been measured at one location in Death Valley—hot enough to fry an egg "over-easy" in just six minutes.

A good method of summing up the combined effects of heat, low humidity, and drying winds is to measure the "potential evaporation" of water from standardized four-foot-diameter pans placed out in the open. At Death Valley the heat and drying winds are capable of vaporizing about 120 inches of water per year—a figure almost 100 times greater than the average annual precipitation. Here, an untended swimming pool could easily dry up in a single summer season. A similar potential evaporation rate exists at the Salton Sea. If not for irrigation runoff from the surrounding Coachella and Imperial valleys, the Salton Sea would probably disappear within a decade.

Winds—the bane of travelers—play an important role in the day-to-day weather of the desert. With little vegetation to dampen the winds, desert breezes tend to pass freely across the open landscapes, often picking up dust as they go. Some winds occur locally and daily due to the presence of nearby mountain ranges—sun-warmed air against the slopes expands and rises, causing cooler air to rush in underneath. But regional air movements often override these local winds. This usually occurs when paired centers of high and low pressure lie on opposite sides of the California Desert—one inland and the other over the Pacific Ocean.

A common situation exists, especially in spring and summer, when a "high" lies offshore over the Pacific, and a "low" centers over Nevada or Utah. Air streaming onshore across the coastal plains funnels into the desert by way of several passes—notably across the low barrier of the Tehachapi Mountains and through San Gorgonio Pass. These are, not coincidentally, prime sites for wind-generated electricity.

When these circumstances are reversed, with high pressure inland and low pressure offshore, a Santa Ana condition occurs. When this happens, most often in fall and winter, moderately warm or even chill but very dry winds sweep westward or southwestward across the desert and race through the mountain passes. Heated by compression while descending toward the coast, this desiccated air produces, for a period typically lasting two or three days, a desert-like climate throughout the southern California coastal plain. Some coastal residents find this shift in the wind irritating. But to others the bright sunshine and clean, dry air are pleasant reminders of the desert lying just beyond the sharp, blue mountains. ◼

Tens of thousands of "snowbirds"—retirees fleeing colder climes—set up winter housekeeping on the California Desert.
BARBARA BRUNDEGE/EUGENE FISHER

The hardy survivors

Under a near-vertical sun the desert bakes and life seems defeated. Yet by summer night or bright spring morning, desert life forges a triumphant, wondrous, often secretive existence.

Unable to adapt to an increasingly harsh environment during the past several thousand years, some species have died out completely. Others have forsaken the desert and withdrawn to more forgiving climes north or west. Still others—more than a thousand plant and half that many animal species—have made peace with the desert environment by evolving physically or behaviorally.

Since plants lack the mobility of animals, they have a somewhat limited repertoire of adaptations. Successful desert plants aren't just simply tough. Most have conjured up clever strategies to deal with the quintessential challenge—limited water. Generalizing, we can conveniently pigeon-hole desert plants into three categories: "avoiders," "tolerators," and "escapers" of drought (recognizing, of course, that many desert plants owe allegiance to more than one of the three).

Avoiders are perennial plants forced to endure the heat and dryness of summer. They can be further described as "water-savers" and "water-spenders."

Cacti and succulent plants, for example, are miserly water-savers. With shallow root systems that collect water during brief periods of rainfall and run-off and thick, waxy skins that hinder evaporation, they have the capacity to hoard water in juicy, ex-

pandable tissues. Some, like the prickly pear, shrivel like a prune, only to double their volume later during a wet spell. Because photosynthesis in these plants is restricted to stems or tiny leaves, they are the "tortoises" of the desert plant world, growing slowly but living long.

The towering saguaro (abundant in Arizona, but present in California in only a few scattered locales near the west bank of the Colorado River) and the

(TOP RIGHT) Rare claret cup cactus rests on a rock ledge in the eastern Mojave Desert. JERRY SCHAD

(RIGHT) The blossoming flower stalk of a desert agave attracts both hummingbirds and bees. LEO L. LARSON

more modest barrel, cottontop, hedgehog, and mound cacti have accordion-like pleats allowing easy expansion. The barrel cactus, which graces upper bajadas and lower mountain slopes from Death Valley to the Mexican border, is renowned in desert legend as a life saver. But don't expect to rely on this cactus—bloated or otherwise—as a ready source of water. When cut open it yields only a bitter, semi-saturated pulp.

Most cactus plants are spine-covered, but not all spiny or thorny desert plants are cactus. On cacti, the spines grow outward from centers on the fleshy stems or pads. The spines are vestigial leaves (some kinds of cacti actually grow tiny, short-lived leaves in addition to spines) that evolved to discourage browsing by animals. The spines also seem to protect the chlorophyll-bearing skin of the cactus from sunlight and drying winds.

The most eye-catching (and the most vicious)

(BELOW) The harmless-looking fuzz packets dotting these beavertail pads are the bane of the curious. Once imbedded in the skin, the tiny spines (called glochids) are almost impossible to remove. CARR CLIFTON

of California cacti are the chollas, especially the teddy-bear, or "jumping," cholla of the Colorado Desert. Backlit by the sun, their densely packed, straw-colored spines glisten and seductively invite tactile exploration. But set within a papery sheath around each spine is an incredibly sharp, microscopically barbed point. At the slightest touch of skin, clothing, or shoe leather, that spine will penetrate and hang on, often taking with it an entire, easily detached, bristling segment of the plant. Experienced desert hikers always carry a comb to help pry away the cholla balls that seem to jump and attach themselves to clothing.

The noncactus succulent plants of the California Desert include the agave, which stores moisture in a rosette of fleshy, spine-tipped leaves, and the elephant tree, whose puffy, water-engorged limbs support rows of ludicrously tiny leaves.

Many cacti and succulents take decades to reach maturity, and then attain only a modest size. Except for the saguaro, the largest California cacti are some varieties of cholla (rarely, up to fifteen feet tall) and the barrel varieties (up to ten feet tall). The most diminutive are various fishhook and foxtail cacti, only a few inches high.

Those plants that have leaves have developed clever water-saving strategies. Some turn their leaves edge-on to the sun, while others roll up or fold their leaves during hot weather to prevent too-rapid transpiration (loss of moisture) during photosynthesis. The spidery ocotillo grows an instant crop of leaves after rainfall, then promptly drops all of them at the first hint of drought.

Unlike water-savers, water-spenders have deeply probing root systems that tap into dependable supplies of water far underground.

Bravely clinging to its perch on solid rock, this young barrel cactus already may have witnessed ten thousand sunsets. Growth takes place in spurts when abundant quantities of water are absorbed through its roots. In drier habitats such as this, the barrel cactus can subsist on stored water alone for several years. CARR CLIFTON

Branches and leaf surfaces are minimized above ground level. Once its water supply is assured, a water-spender can grow year-round.

Probably the most successful water-spender is the mesquite. With a taproot capable of penetrating a hundred feet or more below ground level to reach water percolating down from the mountains, mesquite forms colonies along the edges of washes and in low valleys where water collects underground. It is also an important stabilizer of sand dunes. Drifting sand only encourages new leafy branches to grow upward and outward, while the roots and older branches form a permanent lattice buried in the sand.

(ABOVE) Queen of the desert wildflowers, the desert lily appears only after the right combination of abundant winter rainfall and warm spring sunshine. JERRY SCHAD

(RIGHT) Lipstick-red buds burst forth in glory on the tip of an acotillo branch. Indians used the tangy-sweet blossoms to make a lemonade-like beverage.
JERRY SCHAD

The second major category of drought adapted plants—the tolerators—survive because of physiological adaptations on a cellular or even molecular level. Some have evolved small-sized cells that resist rupture during repeated cycles of shrinkage and expansion. Others can slow their metabolic rates, living off their fat, so to speak, during periods of drought.

The creosote bush, the most abundant and widespread plant species in both the Mojave and Colorado deserts, is an archetypical drought-tolerator. Even though is may react to severe drought by dropping mature leaves and even whole branches, it always retains some of its younger leaves, which will continue manufacturing food by photosynthesis even under the most dire conditions of heat and drought. Creosote bushes, when established, are aggressive competitors for moisture. Their wide-spreading roots often choke out new growth around them, including seedlings of their own species. This process may be aided by toxic substances emitted by the older roots. Because of the cutthroat competition, creosote bushes on the wide, flat surfaces of bajadas assume a uniformly spaced pattern. Seen from a great distance they blend together as a gray or dark green band, often mistaken for a haze along the desert floor.

Other plants that play the role of drought-tolerators, at least part-time, are the smoke tree and palo verde. Both rely on photosynthesis in their

branches and twigs, as they hold on to their tiny leaves for only a short time during the spring. The smoke tree, a dweller of sandy washes, utilizes a reproductive strategy that practically ensures its success on germination. Its seed, coated with a tough, water-impervious substance, sprouts only if it is

tumbled about and abraded by sand in a flash flood. Only under those circumstances will there be enough moisture in the soil to support the early stages of the plant's growth. Once established, it is a tough survivor.

Avoiders and tolerators are the bread and butter of desert vegetation, but escapers are the spice. These plants don't face the harsh reality of the desert head-on; they evade it completely. Surviving in durable seed form for months or years, they lie dormant until the right conditions of moisture and warmth trigger a hurried cycle of germination, growth, flowering, and seed production.

Evaders include annual grasses and colorful ground-hugging wildflowers that are alluring not only because of their extravagant beauty and perfume but also because of their rarity and unpredictability. When the rain and sun gods are benevolent, the sandy flats and the lower hillsides of both California deserts sport carpets of desert sunflower, dune primrose, sand verbena, desert poppy, desert dandelion, and monkeyflower. The western reaches of the Mojave Desert (Antelope Valley, in particular) are famous for springtime displays of coreopsis and

(ABOVE) Often found around desert springs and seeps and in protected crannies, desert phacelia sports purple-blue blossoms arranged around a stem shaped like a fiddlehead. LARRY MINDEN

(RIGHT) Dull and unattractive in drought, the creosote bush brightens up after sufficient rainfall. Miniature yellow flowers are followed by an abundant crop of densely wooly "seed balls"—the fruit of the plant. D. CAVAGNARO

the state flower, California poppy. These poppies, normally restricted to the coastal hills and inland valleys, clearly invaded this area of the desert through the low-elevation passes to the west.

Here and there on mountainsides, flats, and washes alike are hundreds of other wild, flowering plants; among them blazing star, scarlet locoweed, gilia, desert aster, and prickly poppy. Some, like desert mariposa, desert hyacinth, and desert lily, push up through damp earth from underground bulbs.

(RIGHT) This aster's lilac petals provide striking contrast to the desert's rocky mesas. JERRY SCHAD

(BELOW) A decorative but deadly competitor of water-loving native plant species, the nonnative tamarisk grows thick along the banks of the Colorado River. The clusters of tiny pink flowers appear in the spring and last well into summer. KAZ HAGIWARA

Floral displays are most extravagant in late winter and early spring as a consequence of the sparse but dependable winter rains. A second flowering may occur in early fall, especially in the southern and eastern reaches of the California Desert, as a result of capricious late-summer tropical storms.

Aside from the avoiders, tolerators, and escapers of the arid regime, the desert supports certain native plants that have never had to deal with aridity at all. These water-loving, riparian plants—palms, willows, cottonwoods, sycamores, and related undergrowth like ferns and mosses—thrive along the Colorado River, along the rare true desert watercourses, and around perennial springs. These plants and the oasis-like areas that support them provide a vital refuge for animals ill-equipped to tackle the desert environment head-on.

Much of the riparian vegetation consists of "relict" plant species from earlier, moister times. The California fan palm, for instance, may be a holdover from Pleistocene times, when it was perhaps more widely distributed throughout the Colorado Desert area. Today it has retreated to isolated canyons and springs. Only in those places can it stand with its feet in the water and crown in the sunshine.

Several plants we now consider desert natives (including the most ubiquitous of all—the creosote bush) have come to us only in the last ten or twenty thousand years by extension of their ranges north from Mexico. But these natural invasions, which creep along slowly even today, have been augmented—again for thousands of years—by the artificial introduction of species by man.

Some plants, such as desert tobacco, were introduced by the Indians centuries ago but escaped to become harmless, naturalized members of the desert vegetation community. Other more recent arrivals, accidentally or purposefully introduced, have been detrimental. A notorious example is the tumbleweed, or Russian thistle, whose rounded, woody skeletons rolling in the wind and collecting against buildings and fences are evocative of desolate places throughout the West. Another example is the tamarisk, or salt cedar, an Old World native planted in rows to form windbreaks

These coyote tracks were imprinted in desert mud in a wash in the Imperial Valley. As sun and wind suck dry this desert clay, geometric minicanyons appear. ROY MURPHY

around agricultural areas in California and Arizona. One fast-growing type of tamarisk—though handsome enough in appearance—spreads seeds on the wind, colonizes easily wherever water is present, and competes vigorously with other riparian trees—especially willows. It has virtually taken over some desert oases and waterways. Biologists and desert park rangers never seem to tire of yanking out new tamarisk growth in the wild canyons, yet total eradication in the wild seems hopeless.

Some of California's native desert plants have been planted widely elsewhere: the fan palm, used in landscaping, and jojoba, a desert shrub experimentally cultivated in recent years. Jojoba beans yield a high-quality oil used for cosmetics and industrial applications.

Two centuries ago the Yuma and Kamia Indians cultivated maize, squash, and gourds, presaging the agricultural takeover of the Imperial, Coachella, and Palo Verde valleys.

Today vast monocultures of nonnative citrus trees, date palms, and grain and vegetable crops dominate fertile desert soil wherever water is easily available. It could be said that because of irrigation, the California Desert is one of the few in the world that is actually shrinking, while many are expanding due to overgrazing, deforestation, and other causes resulting in desertification, too. The Owens Valley, once lush with grasslands and crops, was transformed into a marginal desert by the almost total appropriation of its water resources by a thirsty Los Angeles.

While desert-adapted plants have been able to confront heat and aridity primarily by physical adaptations, animals have met the challenge largely by altering their behavior. Still, many desert creatures have evolved certain physiological characteristics that have maximized their success at desert living.

One such creature superbly adapted to the desert is the coyote. Although widespread throughout North America, the desert subspecies is paler in color and smaller than those found in coastal or high-

mountain habitats. These omnivorous canines usually hide themselves under low bushes or in mountain crevices during the heat of the day. By twilight or night they are out on the hunt. They prefer fresh meat (especially rabbits and rodents) and sweet fruit or berries (including palm fruit). The coyote is, of course, the desert's most talented vocalist. No evening or dawn on the California Desert is complete without a weird chorus of high-pitched barks, yelps, and wavering howls.

The largest mammal here is the desert bighorn sheep. Once widespread throughout the arid uplands, these shy creatures have retreated to the rugged crags and dry slopes of the most remote desert and desert-bordering mountain ranges. The bighorn population declined sharply in the late 1800s with the introduction of diseases carried by domestic sheep and cattle and unmanaged hunting. Today, though legally protected throughout most of their range, the roughly four thousand desert bighorn sheep in California maintain a precarious existence at best. Poaching, lung diseases, competition for habitat with cattle and wild burros and horses, and the generally harsh natural conditions the sheep must contend with keep their numbers trimmed.

The desert bighorn's tan or gray-brown coloring blends well with its drab surroundings. Mature rams can grow to 250 pounds. Both males and females have a white rump patch and a small dark tail, but only the rams display the trademark of the species—massive, curled horns weighing up to thirty pounds a pair. They use these horns as battering-rams in sparring contests during the rutting season. Ewes have much smaller, swept-back horns.

Desert bighorn are well adapted to survive, if need be, on dormant vegetation, no matter how rough or fibrous. Occasionally they break open a barrel cactus with their horns to reach the moist pulp within, and they may even munch on the fearfully armed joints of the cholla cactus. In winter, green vegetation can completely satisfy the bighorn's water needs, but in summer they must visit a source of open water every day or two.

Bighorn are usually found on or near "escape terrain"—steep, rocky slopes free of dense brush. Here they are supremely capable of evading any predator. Their climbing and leaping abilities are almost beyond belief. Some have been known to leap thirty feet down a steep incline, landing with perfect finesse.

Another large mammal that once wintered in the California Desert (especially in Antelope Valley) is the pronghorn. With the ability to sprint at up to seventy miles per hour, a healthy pronghorn had no trouble evading any predator. But pronghorns, unaccustomed to barriers in their natural open habitat, would not cross or jump over even the most trivial linear obstacles, though they were physically able to do so. Fences and railroads built across the desert migration routs in the late 1880s sealed the pronghorn's fate—death by starvation.

Wild horses and wild burros, descendants of the domesticated animals brought here by ranchers and prospectors, still play a colorful role. But they have fewer friends than enemies these days. Wild burros, particularly, appropriate and destroy habitat that otherwise would support bigger and more diverse populations of native animals. Removing burros for domestication is one strategy to limit their numbers in the wilds.

Curiously, Middle Eastern camels had their brief day in the California sun, too. In 1857 Congress granted thirty thousand dollars for the importation of a herd of dromedaries from the Middle East to establish an "Army Camel Corps" in the Mojave Desert. The program was an immediate failure, and the camels ultimately found their way into circuses, zoos, and private barnyards.

Other large mammals that frequent the California Desert at times are the wide-ranging cats—mountain lions and bobcats. Like the desert coyote,

A roundup of wild burros takes place the old-fashioned way on the open range in Death Valley National Park. Elsewhere, feral burros and cattle have been airlifted from rugged terrain by helicopter. CRAIG AURNESS/WEST LIGHT

the desert bobcat, also known as the desert wildcat or desert lynx, is of a paler coloring than its cousins from the more humid areas of the West.

Smaller mammals include the kit fox, a stealthy hunter of small rodents but possessed of a curiosity about humans (some steal up to a campfire gathering and make themselves quite familiar); the antelope ground squirrel, a chipmunk-like creature that favors the desert foothills; the badger; the desert cottontail rabbit; and the jackrabbit.

The jackrabbit (strictly a hare and not a rabbit) conceals itself in forms—clearings nibbled out of dense shrubs or grass tussocks—during the midday heat, emerging only during the cooler hours to feed on nearby vegetation. With paper-thin, heavily veined ears, the jackrabbit radiates excess heat into the surrounding atmosphere, much like the radiator of an automobile.

Some rodents, like the kangaroo rat, excavate labyrinthine underground galleries. Here they bask in cool comfort during the day while the ground surface bakes at temperatures fifty to a hundred degrees hotter. The kangaroo rat can endure a lifetime without so much as one sip of free water. It absorbs some water from vegetable food, but most of its liquid comes from a metabolic process in which water is synthesized from the chemical components of dry seeds. Its internal supply is always wisely managed: The kangaroo rat seals its burrow during the day to keep the humidity level high and only ventures out at night. The animal's feces are almost totally dry and its urine is extremely concentrated.

Another rodent, the pack rat, travels far and wide to pick up construction materials for its daytime hideaways—cool crevices, caves, and abandoned shacks. Cholla cactus joints are a prized building material; how the pack rat manages to safely transport these wickedly armed spine clusters is an enduring mystery.

Desert reptiles are many and varied, from snakes to lizards to the desert tortoise—a symbol of the Mojave Desert. Protected from water loss by its thick skin and shell, the desert tortoise lumbers across the sandy flats during pleasant weather in search of succulent vegetation. During hot and cold seasons, it retreats into a long burrow, where it bides time in dormancy. It stores excess water in its urinary bladder, but even "on empty," the animal can withstand long periods of dehydration.

The chuckwalla lizard inhabits rocky areas,

(LEFT) Desert bighorn ram sports three-quarter curl horns, indicating an age of six or seven years. JERRY SCHAD

(BELOW) Out and about at midnight, a tiny Merriam's kangaroo rat forages for dry seed or perhaps cookie crumbs left by a less-than-meticulous camper. RICK MCINTYRE

where it frustrates predators by wedging itself into a narrow crevice and inflating its body to prevent removal. But this technique was useless against the predation of desert-dwelling Indians, who considered them a delicacy. They used a sharpened stick to deflate and remove them from the rocks.

The fringe-toed lizard is an amazing sand swimmer. Adapted to areas of fine sand, it wriggles under the surface—both to stay cool and to escape predators. Serrated hind toes increase its traction on top of the sand, while a streamlined shape and slippery skin facilitate its movements below the sand. The lizard's overlapping eyelids and ear flaps protect its eyes and ears, and special nasal valves prevent sand from entering its lungs as it breathes just under the surface.

Of the several varieties of rattlesnakes inhabiting the California Desert, the sidewinder is uniquely adapted to an environment of open sand. It moves by a curious form of sideways locomotion. Tracks left in the sand by a sidewinder take the form of a series of roughly parallel, but diagonally inclined gouges. The sidewinding movement not only assures good traction, it also minimizes the surface area of sand in contact with the snake's body, thus reducing the rate of heat transfer to its body. Few Californians have died from rattlesnake bites, though one species, the Mojave rattlesnake, has an extremely toxic venom capable of causing almost immediate respiratory distress.

The spadefoot toad, named for the sharp-edged projections on its hind feet used for burrowing, lives a dual life of frantic activity and incredible boredom. Since toads lose a lot of moisture through their skins, the spadefoot must spend several months (sometimes several years) underground in a mud-sealed chamber, waiting for the next big downpour. Within an hour after the first soaking rainfall of the season, adult toads climb out from their burrows. Gathering at temporary ponds, they quickly mate and produce eggs that hatch after only a day or two. In two to four weeks, the tadpoles emerge as young adults. Racing against the coming drought cycle, they and the mature toads alike dig in for another long wait.

Most birds who frequent the desert aren't really adapted to it. On the hottest days, they simply fly away to a more pleasant clime. Some species nest in the desert, but they, too, can always escape the worst of the heat by perching in shady spots or well above the heat-radiating ground surface in the tops of small trees.

Hawks, golden eagles, prairie falcons, and ravens range widely across the desert mountains and basins by day, while bats (not birds, of course, but flying mammals) take over the skies at night in quest of flying insects. In canyons and near oases, the hooting of the phainopepla and the liquid trill of the canyon wren break the desert silence.

Few desert-dwelling birds are more carefully protected from predation than the cactus wren, whose nest is set amid the branches of cholla cacti or other formidably armed vegetation. These retreats

Life is a leisurely but serious business for the desert tortoise, whose hard shell protects it from dehydration as well as from attacks by potential predators.
MARK E. GIBSON

are not completely inviolate, though. Owls, squirrels, and small rodents have all been known to overcome the wren's prickly defenses and raid its nest for eggs or young birds.

The roadrunner, the quirky, clownish, ground-dwelling relative of the cuckoo, is not just the fantasy of overly imaginative cartoon script writers. The name comes from its habit of sprinting along roadways when surprised by equestrians or motorists. With its heavy bill, long counterbalancing tail, and

agile movements, it successfully preys upon insects, scorpions, lizards, and snakes (including the rattlesnake, which it dispatches with lightning-quick stabs of the beak).

The poorwill, an inhabitant of desert mountains, exhibits a truly unique form of bird behavior—hibernation. It endures the winter cold spell by seeking out a rocky crypt and then sinking into a comatose state for as long as several weeks. During this time the bird's normal body temperature of 106 degrees may drop to less than 60 degrees.

On the ground itself, but protected from the sunlight in crevices, under rocks, and in pools, dwell a variety of desert insects, arachnids, crustaceans, myriapods, and even mollusks. In the autumn, male tarantulas patrol the open spaces of the desert, looking for mates who like to remain hidden in bur-

(LEFT) A roadrunner proudly displays its latest catch—a small insect. FRANK S. BALTHIS

(BELOW) Keeping a wary eye on the photographer, this jackrabbit is poised to bolt.
STEPHEN J. KRASEMANN/DRK PHOTO

rows. Tarantulas out in the open are subject to attack by a variety of parasitic flies and wasps, including the dreaded "tarantula hawk," a large blue, red, and green wasp that paralyzes the tarantula with venom, then drags it to a special burrow where it serves as live food for the wasp's voracious larval offspring.

Scorpions abound in the desert lowlands, but they are seldom seen because of their secretiveness. The California-dwelling species are only mildly poisonous, unlike a smaller, related species in southern Arizona and Mexico whose venom contains a neurotoxin capable of killing a child.

Sometimes hikers happen upon small, empty snail shells among the rocks and brush of the desert

foothills and mountain summits. A close inspection of the shady, moist microenvironments along rock crevices or under dense shrubbery may even reveal live snails, some barely visible to the naked eye. As farfetched as it may sound, even water snails exist on the California Desert: soft-bodied invertebrates that survive in the shallow, salt-saturated pools of Badwater in Death Valley.

Saline pools and streams throughout many parts of the California Desert also contain species of small fish—pupfish—that have adapted to the changing environment over the past ten thousand years. Although pupfish seem to be descended from common ancestors that once swam freely in the lake and river systems of the late Pleistocene, they have since differentiated into several species, each indigenous to a small aquatic area.

Even so uncompromising a habitat as an ephemeral rain pool can contain thousands of wriggling fairy and tadpole shrimp. The eggs of these tiny crustaceans, encased in the sun-baked mud of a pool's dry bottom, have been known to endure as many as twenty-five years of drought.

If anything, exploration of the California Desert shows us how invasive life is on our planet. Far from being a barren wasteland, of interest only to geolo-

(ABOVE) Static friction keeps the sidewinder from slipping on soft sand. RICK MCINTYRE

(RIGHT) Subterranean life flourishes on sand dunes. Nests of two-inch-long burrowing wasps score the surface of a sand hill at Death Valley National Park. JAMES M. HARRIS/THE PHOTOGRAPHIC EDGE

gists and hard-rock miners, the California Desert is
a living tapestry of biological dependencies. No one
who makes a sincere effort to understand its subtle-
ties can fail to be impressed. ▣

The stitchery of a sidewinder's purposeful path embroiders the velvet-textured sand
in Death Valley National Park. LEWIS KEMPER/DRK PHOTO

California Desert Conservation Area

A desert bighorn ram on a jutting ridge calmly surveys the larger world below. On the creosote-dotted basin he can see and hear strange two-, three-, and four-wheeled vehicles. The glint of reflected sunlight from some metallic construction on the next ridge catches his eye. The ram turns away, but only to a view of more unnatural sights—roads, power lines, microwave relay towers, windmills, salt works, clouds of dust, and fumes from the great unseen cities to the west. Every year his world seems to shrink.

But does the bighorn's home really shrink? Is the march of civilization incompatible with a natural desert? Can it be stopped? Has a balance been struck between the protection of natural values and the human uses of the California Desert? The answer, of course, is controversial.

The issue, at least, has been addressed in a big way. In 1976 Congress created the California Desert Conservation Area (CDCA), drawing political boundaries around virtually all 25 million acres of California's desert and mandating a comprehensive management plan governing its protection and use. The task of preparing the plan fell to the BLM, which administered half of the 25 million acres of the CDCA at that time.

The management plan, completed in 1980, tried to balance the desert's conflicting uses and needs: consumptive uses like mining and energy development, sustained-yield uses like grazing, recreational pursuits ranging from backpacking to off-road-vehicle free play, and stringent protection of some areas for wilderness and wildlife values. The BLM's California Desert Conservation Area Plan was one of the largest regional planning efforts ever undertaken in the United States and elicited much comment and debate. As a result, far more attention than ever was turned toward desert areas outside the popular destinations like Palm Springs, the Colorado River, Death Valley, and Joshua Tree.

Since the enactment of the California Desert Protection Act in 1994, the BLM has relinquished its management responsibilities for some areas. Most notably, Mojave National Preserve is now run by the National Park Service. Even so, more than 9 million acres of the 25-million-acre CDCA remains under BLM jurisdiction.

The BLM tries to inform prospective visitors of the scenic opportunities within its share of the CDCA and also seeks to educate the public concerning the proper uses of the land. Twenty-two "Desert Access Guides"—large-scale topographic maps—covering the entire California Desert have been produced, identifying visitor facilities, points of interest, and more than 40,000 miles of maintained and unmaintained roads. These maps, along with signs posted along the highways and dirt byways, have helped establish a framework for the orderly recreational use and public access for a desert that had long suffered from an "anything goes" attitude by some of its users. Uniformed desert rangers enforce the rules, as well as provide visitor assistance and interpretation of desert features.

The BLM's 1980 Conservation Area Plan established six *national natural landmarks,* thirty-one *natural areas,* and eighty *areas of critical environmental concern.* Since 1994, some of these have been absorbed into the Mojave National Preserve, or into the expanded portions of Joshua Tree and Death Valley national parks. In any case, these specially designated areas deserve special protection because of their historical, cultural, or scenic values; fish or wildlife resources; or other unique natural systems. The following is a summary of these and other no-table attractions in the CDCA generally lying outside the four "big" parks: Mojave, Death Valley, Joshua Tree, and Anza-Borrego.

Nestled in a corner of the vast, empty Saline Valley, this salt marsh hosts a thriving population of fish, amphibians, and mammals. This and dozens of other areas throughout the California Desert noted for their geological, biological, and cultural values have been designated as areas of critical environmental concern by the BLM.

BARBARA BRUNDEGE/EUGENE FISHER

National natural landmarks

The six national natural landmarks of the California Desert are all areas of primarily geological interest. Cinder Cones, which lies along a major entry way into the Mojave National Preserve, is described in the next chapter.

The Rainbow Basin National Natural Landmark near Barstow has long been famous for the fossils of extinct mammals imbedded in its colorful, rapidly eroding sedimentary deposits. Trapped in these ancient lakebeds of ten million to thirty million years ago are the fossilized remains of insects (among the best preserved anywhere) and animals such as camel, mastodon, three-toed horse, rhinoceros, and a large "bear-dog" creature. Nearby Owl

Canyon Campground serves as a good base camp for extended exploration of the area, but no hobby collecting is allowed.

Pinnacles National Natural Landmark (Trona Pinnacles), just south of the dry lakebed of Searles Lake, highlights the most spectacular tufa formations in North America. The tufa (a calcium carbonate deposit) was formed around the vents of hot springs issuing from the floor of the ice-age Lake Searles. Now high and dry, the tufa towers look like soft dried-mud pillars, but they can cut like coral.

North of Death Valley, the Eureka Sand Dunes National Natural Landmark features the 682-foot-high Eureka Dunes, the tallest in California. Rising from the south end of Eureka Valley, the brilliant dunes stand in stark contrast to the dark and rumpled summits of the Last Chance Range behind them.

Amboy Crater, another national natural landmark, is approached along the old U.S. Route 66 south of Interstate 40. The dark, 200-foot-high volcano is an easy half-hour hike over a landscape of sand drifts and tortured lava beds. Climb the steep

(LEFT) Owl Canyon, a part of the Rainbow Basin National Natural Landmark, hides in its corrugated folds a fossil record stretching back millions of years. JEFF D. NICHOLAS

(BELOW) Dry-land sailing craft easily exceed the legal highway speed limit on the many dry lakes in the Mojave Desert. CRAIG AURNESS/WEST LIGHT

slope of the cone directly or walk around to the west side, where a lava flow has breached the wall.

The Imperial (Algodones) Sand Dunes stretch for forty miles east and south of the Salton Sea, forming the most widespread dune field in California. South of Highway 78, the dunes are a popular open area hosting thousands of off-road vehicle enthusiasts on holiday weekends. North of the highway, however, a substantial portion of the dunes is closed to vehicles because of its national natural landmark status. Visitors can, of course, explore that area on foot. ■

The Inyo Mountains, the first range east of the Sierra Nevada, are mantled in winter snowfall. Rising nearly 8,000 feet from their base, the Inyos are one of the largest and most precipitous mountain escarpments in the West. The Saline Valley lies in the middle distance. BARBARA BRUNDEGE/EUGENE FISHER

Natural areas and areas of critical environmental concern

The natural areas and areas of critical environmental concern are too numerous to fully describe or even list in this book. But some of them deserve mention.

Saline Valley, a vast and silent trough separated from the Owens Valley and the Sierra Nevada by the towering Inyo Mountains, is home to isolated warm springs and a big salt playa bordered by a salt marsh that serves local wildlife. The playa was mined for salt and borax around the turn of the century, and an ingenious tramway was constructed to haul the salts over the Inyo Mountains to be milled in the Owens Valley.

At least one canyon in the Inyos west of Saline Valley harbors a perennial desert waterfall—a distinction shared by the better-known Darwin Falls to the south, a short distance off Highway 190 between Owens Valley and Death Valley.

Just a mile's detour from Highway 395 near Little Lake in the southern Owens Valley is Fossil Falls, a tongue of black and blistered basalt sliced through by the restless waters of the ice-age Owens River. Today that river finds its last expression in Owens Lake. In the late Pleistocene, however, the overflow from the lake continued south past the falls area into the drainage of Searles Lake. Left high and dry today, the falls are a maze of water-polished chutes, potholes, and tunnels. Indians found the area much to their liking during periods ranging from hundreds to thousands of years ago. The recent Shoshone Indians left obvious reminders of their presence, including innumerable obsidian flakes—the vast products of arrowhead manufacture.

Due south, near California City, is a 38-square-mile area partly surrounded by a special mesh fence designed to keep out motorized vehicles and livestock. This is the Desert Tortoise Natural Area, the largest preserve for a nongame species in the United States. While desert tortoises once roamed parts of the Mojave Desert in numbers as great as one thousand to the square mile, much of their prime habitat has already been usurped. Collectors have also contributed to their decline. The fence permits free

(BELOW) "The King Clone," one of several large, circular arrangements of creosote bushes discovered on the sandy flats of the Mojave Desert, apparently spread from a single plant which germinated during the close of the last major ice age, more than ten thousand years ago. GALEN ROWELL

passage of the tortoises into or out of the preserve and ensures their safety while in it.

Here, as in other areas such as the Coachella Valley Preserve (protecting native palm oases and a threatened species of fringe-toed lizard) and Big Morongo Preserve north of Palm Springs (protecting a desert-bordered strip of riparian vegetation visited by some 250 species of birds), private organizations such as the Nature Conservancy have assisted the BLM in buying, leasing, or administering properties needed to guarantee ecological integrity.

Johnson Valley, north of the San Bernardino Mountains, is noted for its unusual groupings of rare creosote bush clones—circular arrangements of creosote bushes cloned from the same central plant. Based on the assumed growth rate (a ring of cloned bushes spreads outward about one millimeter per year), some of the clones may date from the end of the Pleistocene, around ten thousand years ago, when creosote bushes were presumably invading the north from arid lands to the south in response to a drying trend in the climate. Biologists now recognize these clones as the world's oldest living organisms—much older than the previous record-holders, the bristlecone pines. A new find, dubbed the "Grandfather King Cone" has just been dated at 13,000 years.

East of Palm Springs, the contorted Mecca Hills draw people like a magnet. Here there's room for all—campers, motorcyclists, and foot travelers. But hikers reap the best rewards—miles of narrow slot canyons, tunnels, and cave-like recesses in these eroded mudstone hills, and an occasional surprise such as a palm oasis.

The Giant Desert Figures Historic Landmark next to the Colorado River near Blythe, on the other hand, is best seen by air. It consists of enormous intaglios or geoglyphs (large, prehistoric images etched into the flat desert floor)—human and animal figures believed to represent creation myths. These are the best known on the California Desert, but others have been discovered near the Mexican border in the southern Colorado Desert. ∎

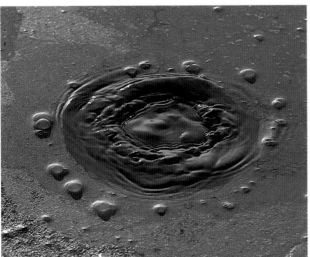

(LEFT, TOP) For untold millennia the dense basalt bedrock at Fossil Falls yielded to the abrasive flow of silt-laden glacial meltwater. Silent now, only an occasional trickle of water flows through this chasm. EDWIN C. ROCKWELL

(LEFT) A mud pot on the southeastern shore of the Salton Sea indicates geothermal activity. PAUL R. JOHNSON

Other public lands

An overview of the CDCA would not be complete without mentioning certain state parks and other public lands within or bordering the conservation area but not administered by the BLM.

The spectacular multihued cliff faces of Red Rock Canyon State Park in the western Mojave are oddly familiar to many first-time visitors. They have been used as a scenic backdrop for countless motion picture and television productions. Like badlands elsewhere, those at Red Rock preserve important sequences of geological as well as paleontological history. Park buffs await the pending acquisition of about twenty thousand acres of adjacent BLM lands, which will beef up the park's somewhat meager holdings.

Saddleback Butte State Park and the Antelope Valley California Poppy Reserve, both located near the sprawling communities of Lancaster and Palmdale, are good places to view springtime displays of wildflowers. Lying a scant one-hour drive from the San Fernando Valley, they represent some of the last untouched desert landscapes in the booming Antelope Valley. In addition to the flowers,

Saddleback Butte has a large area of undisturbed Joshua tree woodland.

The strip of California Desert along the Colorado River lies outside the conservation area, but it is a major draw for weekend recreationists in all seasons. Every conceivable water sport—from motorboating and jet skiing to canoeing, inner tubing, and fishing—is popular here. Remote Picacho State Recreation Area lies on the bank of the river, accessible only by water or by eighteen miles of bone-shaking dirt road. Picacho Peak, a plug-dome volcanic outcrop, presides over the warm-season parade of boaters and swimmers drifting in the languid, turbid waters of the river. North of the recreation area, two small national wildlife refuges—Imperial and Cibola—straddle the river and harbor ducks, geese, and clapper rails.

At the Salton Sea State Recreation Area, anglers could until recently pursue orangemouth corvina, sargo, and gulf croaker—all species of ocean-going fish that were introduced into the briny waters during the fifties. Increasing salinity, however, is poisoning even these salt-tolerant species. The Salton Sea lies in a closed basin and thus releases water only by evaporation. Meanwhile, saline

(RIGHT) Unscreened by vegetation and seldom washed by rain, painted graffiti on desert boulders may last centuries—a dubious legacy for our descendants.
TOM BEAN

runoff from the agricultural region surrounding the sea continues to pour in. Still, duck hunting remains a popular pastime here during the cooler months. The Salton Sea National Wildlife Refuge, along the shallows at the south end of the sea, hosts many species of birds that stop here during migrations along the Pacific Flyway.

With its collection of diverse scenic wonders, land- and water-based recreational attractions, historical sites, mining and industrial installations, and small and large towns, the desert is no longer looked down upon as the poor stepchild of California's geography. The CDCA's far-flung boundaries have created a sense of place for the whole of the California Desert—a place coveted by competing interests, to be sure, but a *place*, nonetheless. With ever-accelerated demands on its resources, the CDCA can only be managed by the careful stewardship of government agencies and committed private citizens with a clear vision of the future. 🔲

The towering battlements of Red Rock Canyon State Park reveal the brute cutting power of water.
JAMES RANDKLEV

Mojave National Preserve

It lies under the scorching sun—vast, empty, inscrutable, and mostly unrecognized by motorists gliding along Interstate 15 between Los Angeles and Las Vegas. Those few who tear their attention away from the mesmerizing line of dots on the pavement may catch sight to the south of a desolate but oddly intriguing landscape of glistening salt flats, coal-black lava beds, rumpled sand dunes, and purple ridge after purple ridge.

This is the eastern Mojave, the antithesis of the bustling, space-age western Mojave Desert. Dominated by crags of limestone, dolomite, rhyolite, and granite; awash in basins of sediment; and bristling with the ubiquitous denizens of the high desert—the Joshua tree and the Mojave yucca—the 1.4-million-acre Mojave National Preserve is a place of serene beauty and unexpected discovery.

Modern civilization has touched the eastern Mojave in many ways but has never dominated it. Almost ten thousand mining claims are on file in the preserve, yet only four mines are now active—two cinder quarries, one clay mine, and one gold mine. Two freeways, Interstates 15 and 40, pass along its borders, and a major railroad runs across its midsection, yet roadways in its interior remain largely unpaved. High-voltage power lines, telephone cables, and gas and oil pipelines snake through some of its valleys and passes, but other areas are completely free of any sign of humans.

For the five hundred or so residents of the eastern Mojave region—mostly ranchers, miners, and railroad employees—the Old West is not so much a memory as a reality. Windmills on the lonely flats creak and groan as they pull up niggardly amounts of water for thirsty cattle. Cowboys wield branding irons at roadside corrals. Elderly prospectors still search for a bit of color amid their mining claims.

The eastern Mojave is a desert of mountains and sweltering basins. Sixteen mountain ranges in all stand within the preserve, some rising cliff-like to heights of one mile above the surrounding flats. Three general alignments of mountain ranges are discernible from the air as a consequence of underlying fault patterns, but from the ground the arrangement of both mountains and basins seems quite random. The geological history of the area is a long and complex one: the rocks exposed here range in age from more than one billion years (in the case of some outcroppings near the Providence Mountains) to less than a thousand years (the cinder cones and lava flows near Baker).

Because of its position in the geographic center of the Mojave Desert (both California's and Nevada's), eastern Mojave serves as a kind of bo-

It's branding time at the Blair Ranch in the Mojave National Preserve. These activities maintain a hundred-year tradition that began with the discovery that livestock and animals pulling wagons along the Mojave Road could thrive on the rich rangelands of Cima Dome and Lanfair Valley. CRAIG AURNESS/WEST LIGHT

tanical crossroads. Here, for example, the smoke tree and palo verde—normally found in the Sonoran Desert—have leapfrogged north to make scattered appearances at the lower elevations. The Great Basin sage (purple sage), on the other hand, has crept south from its normal dwelling places in eastern California and northern Nevada to invade a few of eastern Mojave's higher valleys. Largely, however, the typical Mojave Desert flora predominates—creosote and bur sage in the low basins, Joshua-tree woodland on middle-elevation basins and plateaus, cactus in the rocky alluvial fan and slopes, and pinyon-juniper forest wherever the mountains reach 4,000 or 5,000 feet or more.

The Mojave National Preserve is the intrepid explorer's dream. Facilities, improvements, and people are few, but opportunities for discovery are everywhere. With a full tank of gas (none is available inside the preserve's perimeter), and five or more gallons of water, you're free to wander along dozens of archaeological and historical sites, and old mines. Foot travel takes you still farther.

Staying overnight? Just roll out the bedroll and sleep under the stars. Only three developed campgrounds (Hole-in-the-Wall, Mid Hills, and at Mitchell Caverns) serve overnighters, yet several other sites are available for no-facilities car- or tent-camping. Backpackers are free to camp virtually anywhere, except near roads and springs.

Not to be missed, even on a quick swing through the preserve, are the mysterious Kelso Sand Dunes.

In the silent, fading afterglow of evening, the full moon climbs above Kelso Dunes and the Providence Mountains. Kelso Dunes and parts of a vast, sandy stretch to the west—the Devils Playground—are closed to vehicle use because of possible deleterious effects on dune-dwelling animals and rare plants. DAVID MUENCH

The sand here is a rare type known as "booming" because of its tendency to hum or boom when in motion. About six hundred feet high, the dunes are some of the tallest in North America—but not quite as tall as the Eureka Dunes northwest of Death Valley. The heart-pounding trudge to the top of the highest dune crest is more than worth it for the view.

East of the Kelso Dunes, the pinyon-dotted, brick-red, rhyolite crags of the Providence Mountains stand a vertical mile above the surrounding terrain. Along the eastern slope an older, lower-lying limestone formation is honeycombed with caverns—the result of flooding by acidic water some twelve million years age. Today, of course, these caverns at the Providence Mountains State Recreation Area (Mitchell Caverns Natural Preserve) stand high and dry. On ranger-guided tours, two of the most accessible caves may be explored in some detail. Only one in forty thousand caverns have all three of the major types of formations found here: dripstones (the familiar stalactites and stalagmites), flow stones (curtains and draperies), and erratics (shields and tubes). Just outside the caverns, the panorama to the east and south reveals an empty expanse of desert floor big enough to swallow the city of Los Angeles. On the clearest days, the Hualapai Mountains of Arizona seem to float on a horizon almost a hundred miles away.

North of the Mitchell Caverns is Hole-in-the-Wall country, symbolized by the "Swiss cheese" rocks adjoining the campground there. Shaped by wind and water, these grotesque outcrops of volcanic breccia are breached at one spot by a steep, narrow passage leading down to a spooky amphitheater called Banshee Canyon. Iron rings set in the rock assist agile and not-so-agile climbers alike.

Along nearby Wildhorse Canyon, another tortured outcrop of pitted rock rises from the sandy desert floor. Amid the heap of boulders at its base is the stylized art of long-departed Indians. Above the fading petroglyphs and pictographs an eerie aperture invites exploration. Here, it seems, Indians wriggled through the hole in rebirth ceremonies. The rock is worn glassy smooth from thousands of passages.

North of Hole-in-the-Wall, the road ascends to the pinyon- and juniper-covered tablelands and canyons of the Mid Hills—part of a continuous upland that includes the Providence Mountains in the south and the New York Mountains in the north.

(TOP RIGHT) Illuminated by electric lights and dry as a bone, Mitchell Caverns are quite unlike dank limestone caves found elsewhere. MARK E. GIBSON

(RIGHT) Dirt bikers at Dove Springs in the Mojave Desert ponder the next move. More than a half million acres have been reserved for vehicle free play and exploration in the CDCA. SUZI MOORE

Amid the Manhattan-like turrets on the summit ridge of the New Yorks, bighorn sheep survey what remains of their once-exclusive domain.

Through the heart of the Mid Hills and bisecting the preserve east-west is one of the most significant historical routes in California—the Mojave Road. Largely traceable today by four-wheel-drive vehicle, and in part only by foot, this old wagon road evolved from an ancient Indian trade route from the Colorado River to the Pacific coast. The Spanish missionary Francisco Garces (a veteran of the first Anza expedition in 1774) crossed the desert by this route in 1776; and numerous Americans, including Jedediah Smith and Kit Carson, used the trail in the early 1800s. The U.S. Army transformed the trail into a wagon road in the late 1850s. It then had steady use by the military, the postal service, and the wagon trains of the California emigrants. This Government Road was as important in its day as Interstate Highways 40 and 15 are to us today.

There is hardly a more fascinating hike in the preserve than the hardscrabble trek down Piute Hill.

This section of the Mojave Road, crossing the Piute Range, had the reputation of being one of the worst ordeals on Western trails. Here, among glistening cholla and ruddy barrel cacti and somber green yuccas, the deep ruts of wagon wheels worn into volcanic rock are still visible. Along the way are fragments of the original Indian trail that preceded the wagon tracks, marked by petroglyphs inscribed on the smooth-faced boulders. A veritable oasis lies at the bottom of the grade—a mile-long ribbon of willows, cottonwoods, and other riparian vegetation fed by Piute Spring. On a rocky bluff above the creek stand the crumbling stone walls of Fort Piute, a Mojave Road way station manned by the U.S. Army from 1866 to 1867.

Farther west along the Mojave Road is Lanfair Valley, the site of an early-century experiment with agriculture. The homesteaders who were producing

Volcanic rock, sculptured by wind and water, forms the backdrop of Hole-in-the-Wall campground in Mojave National Preserve. BARBARA BRUNDEGE/EUGENE FISHER

bumper crops of wheat and barley during a freak wet cycle after World War I saw their hopes turn to dust when the normal weather pattern returned. In a tragic epilogue—a relay of the classic Western conflict over limited water resources—two men were killed in a shootout at nearby Government Holes in 1925. Today Lanfair Valley's abundant perennial and annual grasses support a sizable herd of cattle.

Visits to Kelso and Cima, tiny whistle-stops along the Union Pacific Railroad, are also rewarding. A small store is located at Cima—the only place to pick up supplies within the preserve. In Kelso there's a pseudo-Spanish-style depot (now awaiting restoration as a possible research and visitor center) that for more than six decades served as a way station for the traveling public and railroad personnel. During World War II, Kelso was home to nearly two thousand people, most connected with the then-active Vulcan iron mine nearby.

North of Cima is the Cima Dome, a symmetrical bulge of weathered granite seventy-five square miles in area and fifteen hundred feet high. One of the outstanding geological structures in the world, this little-understood blister on the earth rises so gently that its form is imperceptible unless viewed from a distance. The dome supports an extensive Joshua tree forest that some believe to be the finest anywhere. A new two-mile-long hiking trail leads from a trailhead on Cima Road to Teutonia Peak, a jagged mass of igneous rock poking upward from Cima Dome's smooth surface. As you walk around the outcrops, your gaze encompasses hundreds of square miles of surrounding desert landscape.

Castle Peaks in the New York Mountains are notable for their diverse vegetation and prime bighorn sheep habitat. The mountain range is specially managed by the BLM as an area of critical environmental concern.
JEFF GNASS

Hundreds of miles of lonely dirt roads thread through the Mojave National Preserve. CRAIG AURNESS/WEST LIGHT

North of Kelso, the road to Baker—Kelbaker Road—passes near an area of desolate lava beds. About thirty cinder cones, some less than a thousand years old, poke up amid extensive lava flows. Dotted with Joshua trees and several varieties of cactus, Cinder Cones National Natural Landmark shows how quickly vegetation can reestablish itself even on marginal soils in a desert climate.

To the west, touching the edge of the busy crossroads town of Baker, is Soda Dry Lake, a twelve-mile-long expanse of salt-frosted playa. On the west shore is Soda Springs—formerly a way station on the Mojave Road, and then a siding for a short-lived railroad, called the Tonopah and Tidewater, although it never reached either one. In the fifties, a resort called Zzyzx Mineral Springs was developed here by radio evangelist Dr. Curtis Howe Springer. Today the old resort grounds are occupied by a desert research station operated by a consortium of seven California State University campuses. A spring-fed pond and nearby marshes serve as protected habitats for the rare Saratoga Spring pupfish and the Mojave chub.

Just north of the big rare earth mine at Mountain Pass (north of Interstate 15) is Clark Mountain, a rugged outcrop of limestone and dolomite rising like a beacon to an elevation of almost eight thousand feet. Set amid a steep, shady bowl north of the summit, a battered grove of white firs struggles for survival. These trees, along with some smaller groves in the New York Mountains to the south and the Kingston Mountains to the north are relicts from the wetter past when conifer forests ranged widely over the mountains of the Mojave Desert.

For the hurried traveler, the "lonesome triangle" of the eastern Mojave is merely a blank and tedious stretch just beyond the shoulder of the interstate freeway—a wasteland not even worth contemplating. If you're curious, however, the Mojave National Preserve gives of its treasures. All it requires is that you take the exit ramp and leave the rat race behind. ▣

Musical sands of the Mojave

A roar. A buzz. A hum. The sound of a foghorn or of a low-flying propeller-driven aircraft. The sound of bumble-bees or of kettle drums or of low notes played on a pipe organ or bass violin. These and other noises only impre-cisely describe the truly unique vibrations both heard and felt on the sliding slip faces of the "booming" Kelso Dunes in the Mojave National Preserve.

Once thought to be quite rare, booming sand is now known to be fairly common in large dunes, and at least forty sites are known worldwide. (In the U.S. in addition to the Kelso Dunes, the Eureka Dunes near Death Valley and three dune fields in Nevada exhibit booming effects.) But the Kelso Dunes are among the most musical. When conditions are best—dry sand and warm, dry weather—enterprising and athletic "musicians" can play notes like staccato blasts on a tuba by jumping off the crest of a dune and landing on the steep incline below. More amazing yet are the sounds that result from contin-uous flows of sand down the slip faces. Creative players can trigger these avalanches by pushing sand down with hands or feet, by sledding down on the backside, and by literally swimming downslope using the crawl or breaststroke.

In the deserts of the Middle East and Asia, where massive avalanches of booming sand can occur spontaneously, old legends and traveler's tales spoke of the "song of the desert," variously attributed to the groaning of subterranean deities, the beating of drums in underground caverns, and the chiming of bells in sand-drowned monasteries. Today's more sober scientific explana-tions depend on the physics of moving sand particles.

Geophysicists discovered important clues when individual sand grains from booming and nonbooming sand dunes were examined under a scanning electron microscope. Booming sand particles turned out to be much rounder and better polished than ordinary sand particles. The noises originate as weak vibrations produced by colliding grains when sand layers slip downward. These vibrations are then amplified by the stationary sand underneath, which acts as a giant sounding board.

The Kelso Dunes were built up of sand grains blown in from the Mojave River Sink, about thirty-five miles to the west. Rolled and tumbled across the wastes of the Devils Playground, the grains acquired the neces-sary roundness and polish to produce the eastern Mojave's own song of the desert. ∎

The curious sliding flow of sand at Kelso Dunes suggests a mechanism for the strange booming noises it makes.

JERRY SCHAD

Death Valley National Park

Death Valley. A foreboding trench tucked away in the least populated corner of California. An empty, salt-frosted plain lying lower than sea level. Where summer temperatures routinely compete with the hottest ever recorded. Where aridity rivals the Sahara. Where people are irrelevant, and the rest is seemingly forsaken by God and the living alike.

But there's more to Death Valley National Park than its grim reputation. Within its boundaries mountain ranges soar as high as 11,000 feet above sea level. Rock formations dating almost halfway back to the origin of the earth itself lie exposed in the sun. And diverse biological habitats, from alkali flat to pinyon-juniper woodland, support nearly fifteen hundred species of plants and animals. Death

(BELOW) Its name inspired by Dante's description of purgatory in the *Divine Comedy*, Dantes View surveys more than a thousand square miles of tortured metamorphic escarpments, thirsty alluvial fans and bajadas, and lifeless salt flats. DAVID MUENCH

Valley National Park is a 3.3 million-acre, 170-mile-long, open-air museum. The park's present architecture is largely the result of relatively recent geological events. During the last three million years, the mountains flanking the valley—the towering Panamint Range and the more modest Amargosa Range—have risen dramatically, while a long, narrow block of the earth's crust—the bedrock under the valley itself—has sagged between them. Meanwhile, alternate freezing and thawing and other erosive effects have shattered the exposed rocks in the mountains, allowing the smaller pieces to be swept away during floods. The mountain summits have become blunted, and sediments have piled up to a depth of some eight thousand feet over the bedrock floor of Death Valley.

The Pleistocene ice ages also made an important mark on Death Valley. Whenever glaciers retreated from the eastern slope of the Sierra Nevada and the slopes of certain smaller ranges in southern California and southern Nevada, meltwater coursed through a network of streams and lakes with one common destination: Death Valley. During the last such episode, around twenty thousand years ago, the valley filled to a depth of about six hundred feet, forming "Lake Manly." Afterward, as the climate warmed and became much drier, water levels in the lakes dropped, leaving high and dry many of the connecting streams. Lake Manly and most of the other lakes soon evaporated, leaving only horizontal terraces marking their fluctuating shorelines and the brilliant white precipitates of soluble minerals as salt pans in the basins.

Since Lake Manly's demise, rare episodes of flooding temporarily have filled Death Valley with water again. About two thousand years ago the water level in the basin reached a depth of thirty feet, an event that radically reworked the previously deposited salt crust. Most recently, in 1969, steady winter rains and a sudden thaw in the snow-capped

(RIGHT) Schools of tiny pupfish dart about in the shallow, tepid waters of Cottonball Marsh, on the floor of Death Valley. This particular species of pupfish, one of nine in the Death Valley area, can tolerate water five times saltier than sea water. RICK MCINTYRE/DVNM

(BELOW) Another species of pupfish in Death Valley, indigenous to Salt Creek, leads a not-very-private existence beneath a boardwalk traveled by hundreds of people every day. DAVID HISER/PHOTOGRAPHERS ASPEN

Panamints created a two-foot-deep pond covering fifty thousand acres; that pond did not, of course, survive the following summer season.

Death Valley's low position among neighboring mountains and valleys has made it the accidental recipient of extra moisture—not as rain, but as groundwater seeping across rock strata from as far away as the Spring Mountains of Nevada (the third range east of Death Valley). This groundwater emerges in the form of spring-fed pools and tiny streams. It waters the golf course at the Furnace

Creek oasis and in some places supports schools of pupfish, the hardy descendants of fish trapped in Lake Manly. Some pupfish tolerate water up to five times saltier than sea water and water temperatures as high as 111 degrees.

The archaeological record in the Death Valley area shows evidence of four separate Indian cultures, each of which was at least partly influenced by the changing climate. The earliest dates back to about ten thousand years ago, when the region was blessed with the cooler, wetter climate associated with the end of the last ice age and plentiful supplies of plant foods and game. The most recent was the Desert Shoshone culture that arrived about one thousand years ago. They were seasonal nomads who adapted to the by-then hot and dry climate by exploiting food sources both on the valley floor and in the high Panamint Mountains.

(ABOVE) Spectacular Red Wall Canyon slices across the flank of the Grapevine Mountains in Death Valley National Park. TOM BEAN

(TOP RIGHT) A tarantula plods over coarse sand in a dry wash. Relatively mild mannered, most tarantulas will easily tolerate handling by humans. JERRY SCHAD

(RIGHT) The giant hairy scorpion is one of the largest scorpions found in the United States, attaining a length of more than five inches. Virtually all scorpions found in California are relatively harmless to people, having venom little more potent than that of a bee or wasp. RICK MCINTYRE

In December 1849 the first wave of gold seekers peered down upon Death Valley. For these lost emigrants, who were attempting to follow a supposed shortcut to the California goldfields, Death Valley and the formidable wall of the Panamints beyond were simply the last straw. Differences of opinion split the party. All except one person survived, but everyone suffered severe hardships before being rescued or finding a way out. Credit for Death Valley's enduringly morbid name seems to go to one of these rescued pioneers, who, on glancing back at the shimmering salt pan, muttered, "Goodbye, Death Valley."

In the closing decades of the 1800s and during the early 1900s, Death Valley swarmed with miners. Thousands passed in and out of the region, hoping for a big strike or otherwise just living the free-spirited life. Boom cycles persisted for as little as a few months or as long as several years, fueled by discoveries of gold, silver, copper, lead, and borax.

With the creation of Death Valley National Monument in 1933, people began to look upon the area as a vast natural museum housing everything from geological and biological exhibits to artifacts ranging from crude stone tools to rusting relics of the mining days. The sprawling saline basin and formidable mountain barriers that so repelled the early travelers today attract more than a half million visitors every year.

In today's Death Valley National Park, shifting sand dunes, narrow canyons, desolate badlands, oasis-like springs, and the sites of once-bustling mines and mining towns are easy to explore, only a short distance from a parked car. A network of paved and unpaved roads makes this possible, although distances can be deceiving. It may take the better part of a day just to drive from one corner of the park to the other. Well-equipped hikers have within their range literally millions of acres of primitive backcountry in the monument and adjoining its border.

Short of flying over the park, a visitor can enjoy amazing views of the valley and its surroundings from either of two spectacular overlooks. One, a

(TOP RIGHT) Gamely defiant of wind, snow, and drought, a bristlecone pine clings to life on the northeastern slope of Telescope Peak.
EDWIN C. ROCKWELL

(RIGHT) An old Indian hunting blind in the Panamint Range recalls the hunter-gatherer culture prevalent in the California Desert little more than a century ago.
EDWIN C. ROCKWELL

drive-up viewpoint called Dantes View in the Amargosa Range just east of Death Valley, provides a pseudo-aerial perspective including both the dazzling white salt pan of Badwater Basin, almost six thousand feet below, and the massive swell of the Panamint Range, often capped with a brilliant mantle of snow.

The other panorama, from the 11,049-foot summit of Telescope Peak, the crown of the Panamints, is even more complete: the great trough of Death Valley lies eleven thousand feet below, while blue-tinted mountain ranges march along the horizon like giant caterpillars—50, 100, and even 150 miles away. The trek to this viewpoint is a long day's adventure—first by a narrow road leading past the famous Charcoal Kilns in Wildrose Canyon (used more than a century ago to produce charcoal for smelters in the adjacent Argus Mountains), then by seven miles of rough hiking trail leading along the ridges of the Panamint Range to Telescope Peak's bristlcone-pine-clad summit.

Zabriskie Point, arguably the park's most famous if not all-inclusive viewpoint lies just a few miles southeast of the park's Furnace Creek tourist headquarters. From here the yellow-tinted clay hills at the base of the Amargosa Range frame Death Valley's shimmering floor, with the Panamint Range forming a somber backdrop.

The runoff from a rare storm forms sheet flows across Death Valley's salt pan in this panorama from Dantes View.
DAVID MUENCH

Bird's-eye views aside, no one can claim intimacy with the Death Valley region except by experiencing its many wonders at close range. A good place to start is by way of a lonely, rough dirt road leading west from Highway 127 along the desolate Amargosa River at the southern tip of the park. This salt-encrusted wash, with no more than a few scattered pools of alkaline water, drains an amazing four million acres of arid lands along the California-Nevada border. Once brimming with glacial meltwater, its present predicament is nicely summed up by the name of one of its upper tributaries—Thirsty Canyon.

(BELOW) A Neapolitan swirl of minerals exposed at Artists Palette inspires painters as well as photographers.
DAVID MUENCH

The dusty road following the Amargosa River closely traces the exit route of Harry Wade, whose small splinter party of '49ers succeeded in escaping Death Valley with their wagon intact—the only group to do so. Their strategy of turning south and outflanking the mountain barriers enabled them to regain the main Spanish Trail route they had departed from earlier. For them, nothing was lost but precious time.

Near the Ibex Hills, along the southern end of the forbidding Amargosa Range, lies a remarkable triad of fresh-water pools—Saratoga Springs. The ponds are a seasonal habitat for migratory birds and harbor one of the several varieties of pupfish native to the region. On a quiet day, the unrippled surfaces of the pools reflect the blackness of the hills to the east and the seamless blue of the sky.

Up ahead, near where the dirt road joins the paved scenic highway, which runs along the eastern side of Death Valley, and Highway 190, which climbs east over Jubilee and Salsberry passes, a volcanic bluff called Shoreline Butte rises abruptly from the floor of the basin. Etched on its slopes are marks left by the changing levels of the ancient Lake Manly.

North of Shoreline Butte, the scenic highway winds back and forth along the bases of several classically symmetrical alluvial fans. Material forming these fans has spilled from the mouths of several jagged gorges cut into the flanks of the Black Mountains. The surfaces of these fans are so porous that only the most drought-adapted plants, like creosote bush, desert holly, and desert trumpet, survive.

Across the valley at the foot of one of the broad alluvial fans at the base of the brooding panamints is Bennetts Well. Here the Bennett-Arcan party, the last remnant of the lost '49er emigrants, holed up for over three weeks while Manly and Rogers, the two strongest members of the group, groped their way overland, found help at a ranch near Los Angeles, and finally returned to rescue them.

Farther north, nestled in an embayment of the Black Mountains, are the famous Badwater pools. The placid surfaces of these saline springs reflect Telescope Peak some eighteen miles to the west. A soft-bodied saltwater snail, indigenous only to the valley floor, is found here, as well as certain beetles and soldier fly larvae. At night, wolf spiders scurry across the rock-hard salt flats on the margins of the pools. The elevation is 279.6 feet below sea level, only about two feet higher than the

two separate spots on the floor of Badwater Basin—both several miles away—identified as the Western Hemisphere's lowest spot elevations.

North of Badwater, the Black Mountains are composed partly of soft clay deposits derived from ancient lakebed sediment and harder mudstone and siltstone. Colorful mineral deposits and bizarre geological formations caused by rapid

(TOP LEFT) Variegated rock formations mark the upper reaches of Titus Canyon. SCOTT WALDIE

(LEFT) Oasis of creature comforts, the inn at Furnace Creek draws an international clientele. TOM BEAN/DVNM

erosion are the norm. The one-way Artists Drive loop road allows a close-up look at one multicolored hillside dubbed the Artists Palette, where an unusual mosaic of red, yellow, orange, green, violet, brown, and black hues has been caused by oxidation of iron, magnesium, and other minerals. Nearby, in the warm light of late afternoon, the siltstone and mudstone of Golden Canyon seem to glow from within.

On the valley bottom opposite Artists Palette is a miles-long swath of jagged salt pinnacles called the Devils Golf Course. These hummocks and ridges of rock salt were precipitated out when the last big temporary lake dried up about two thousand years ago. Since then, rainfall has partially dissolved the crust of salt, leaving a frosting of needle-like spires rigid and sharp enough to tear shoe leather. Listen closely and you may hear the delicate crackle of expanding salt crystals as the morning sun warms the hard crust.

Up the road a few more miles is Furnace Creek, where, in addition to the golf course, there are hotels, shops, campgrounds, the visitor center, a borax museum, and the ruins of the Harmony Borax Works.

North of Furnace Creek, a short spur road leads to a boardwalk trail traversing Salt Creek and the surrounding alkali marsh. During spring and summer, schools of pupfish dart about in the shallow brackish water. The Salt Creek drainage covers 1.4 million acres within and beyond the northern reaches of the park, but only here does water rise

above the surface as a small stream. Two miles upstream from the boardwalk area, the flowing water tumbles off a small precipice—America's only below-sea-level waterfall.

Perched squarely in the broadest part of Death Valley, just north of Salt Creek, is a remarkable fifteen-square-mile expanse of sand dunes. The source of the sand is the Cottonwood Mountains to the west and northwest, where light-colored particles like quartz and rarer, dark-colored particles like magnetite have been weathered away from rocks and swept together by winds. These "sub-barchans," or modified-crescent-shaped dunes, are quite stable because the winds tend to cancel out here. Sturdy mesquite trees grow in some of the interdune troughs.

The nearby resort village and campgrounds at Stovepipe Wells serve as a jumping-off point for explorations into two of Death Valley's most picturesque canyons—Mosaic and Grotto canyons—where ancient episodes of erosion have assembled intricate "mosaics" of varying rock types and where more recent flows of water have created narrow defiles, dry waterfalls, and shady grottos.

North of the dunes, the highway gains elevation while continuing along the eastern side of Death Valley. In the Grapevine Mountains (the northern

The explosion pit of a geologically recent volcano, Ubehebe Crater still has barren walls after the passage of four thousand years.

JEFF D. NICHOLAS

end of the Amargosa Range), several deep canyons slash back through ancient metamorphosed sediments. The best known of these, Titus Canyon, is threaded by a rugged auto route allowing the motorist (or hiker) an intimate view of the eroded variegated rock layers exposed on the cliff-like canyon walls.

Two big attractions lie at the northern end of Death Valley: Scotty's Castle and Ubehebe Crater. Scotty's Castle, ensconced in the narrow folds of Grapevine Canyon like some expatriated Santa Barbara mansion, was built during the twenties as a winter retreat for the reclusive Chicago millionaire Albert Johnson. A somewhat bizarre relationship developed between Johnson and the thoroughly colorful character "Death Valley Scotty," a sometime cowboy, mule teamster, prospector, teller of tall tales, and publicity hound of national repute. Johnson apparently enjoyed pulling the strings behind Scotty, paying him in secret while allowing him to brag in public about "his" own castle and "his" fabulously rich, hidden gold mine. The National Park Service eventually acquired the castle, and today it is among the most popular attractions in the park.

Ubehebe Crater and its smaller cousin, Little Hebe Crater, were created when rising magma came into contact with groundwater. The resulting steam explosion blew off overlying layers of sedimentary rock and scattered dust and cinders over a wide area. The Ubehebe event, which occurred some four thousand years ago, excavated a pit nearly a half mile wide and five hundred feet deep. Little Hebe's age is estimated at only one thousand years. Surrounding both craters is an otherworldly landscape as black as coal, relieved only by the brave appearance of scattered creosote bush and desert holly.

Beyond the craters a long, gravelly stretch of road rises to a broad pass at nearly 5,000 feet elevation, where Joshua trees survive on stony soil near the northern limit of their range. Eventually, the road leads to the dead-level Racetrack Playa, the depository of fine clay particles washed down from the surrounding Cottonwood Mountains. The so-called Grandstand, actually the erosion-resistant top of a mountain literally buried to its neck in sediment, pokes above the northern end of the playa.

A stroll across the sun-fired, stone-hard clay surface of the Racetrack is a unique and instructive experience. Although nothing really moves or changes here by the hour or the day, a sense of movement pervades all. The endlessly repeated pattern of mud cracks mimics the wind-rippled surface of a lake. Tiny waves seem to caress the Grandstand. Sloping sheets of alluvium being cast off nearby mountainsides seem poised to slide.

Scattered on the surface of the playa are rocks, from

A Moorish mansion with 18 fireplaces and a 185-foot swimming pool in the middle of one of the world's most desolate deserts? Why not? Scotty's Castle is enjoyed by hundreds of thousands of tourists every year.
MARK E. GIBSON

fist size to small boulders, all lying at the end of straight, curved, or even bent tracks preserved in the hardened clay. Scientists conclude the rocks are propelled across the playa by a peculiar combination of strong winds and a slick, wet, or possibly icy surface. Strangely, no one yet has visually confirmed this theory.

Like the moving rocks that no one has ever seen, Death Valley's deepest mysteries are cloaked in a veil of secrecy that only the most patient and inquiring minds can penetrate. In a similar way, the stark appearance of this land is but a mask shown to the casual observer. Its beauty is revealed to those who are both curious and open-minded. ▨

A ghostly trace frozen in clay dogs a boulder on the floor of Racetrack Playa. JERRY SCHAD

The twenty-mule teams of Death Valley

One factor in the success of any mining venture, naturally, is getting the product to market. During the borax boom in Death Valley a century ago, this was especially important. Between the borax works and the nearest railhead at Mojave lay 165 miles of dusty wagon road across some of the West's most desolate landscapes.

The use of huge mule-drawn wagons proved to be an economical solution. Each wagon had front wheels five feet high, rear wheels seven feet high, and a sixteen-foot-long bed capable of carrying a ten-ton load of refined borax. A single such wagon, empty, weighed nearly four tons. Normally, two wagons, plus a third hauling as much as 1,200 gallons of water, were hitched together, collectively amounting to a moving load of some thirty-six tons.

This enormous mass was pulled by teams consisting of two columns of ten mules each. Guided by the driver and a single assistant, these twenty-mule teams and their precious cargoes took only ten days to cross the mountains and desert basins between Death Valley and Mojave. Despite nearly unbearable temperatures, water holes fifty miles apart, and steep, hard-packed downgrades where brake failure could have spelled death for human and equine crew alike, the mule teams managed to deliver their loads punctually for a full five years—1883 to 1888.

Today, three of the original ten sets of borax wagons are on display—two at Furnace Creek in Death Valley National Park and one at the visitor facility next to the borate pit in Boron. All three are still in working order. ∎

ILLUSTRATIONS COURTESY U.S. BORAX

A summer's day in Death Valley

A warm, reddish glow touches the highest peaks of the Panamint Range. The glow expands, intensifies, turns a bright orange, and then begins sinking down the slopes, displacing the blue-tinted night. Within minutes the mountains are in the full grip of a piercing, yellowish-white light.

On reaching the floor of Death Valley, the line between light and shadow races eastward, only to slow again as it approaches the Amargosa Range. The 90 degree coolness of a July dawn dissolves under intense, white sunshine.

Coyotes, foxes, and kangaroo rats take refuge in dens or under dense clumps of vegetation. However, the roads of Death Valley come to life. All day long, test cars pound the pavement. (After thousands of miles of road testing, these hard-driven machines are packed off to factories for disassembly and critical inspection.) The test drivers pass the days and miles in relative comfort, insulated from the savage heat by air-conditioners working, naturally, at full-blast.

Sightseers brave the roads, too. Many are Europeans on summer vacation who are attracted to Death Valley by the inviting-looking green patch on the road map midway between Yosemite and Las Vegas. Other road warriors, an exceedingly rare few, challenge themselves on bicycles or on foot. Over the years several endurance runners and adventurous hikers have traveled the length of the valley on foot in July or August. One runner, aided by a helpful crew doling out water, covered a course 124 miles long in a scant 55 hours.

But if anyone at all truly understands the full ramification of human existence in Death Valley, it is the relative few who have chosen to live and work there year-round—mostly park rangers, administrative and maintenance personnel, hotel and resort operators and staff. They have learned to make peace with the desert during its most extravagant excesses, even if that means passing endless hours in air-conditioned buildings. They know exactly what it's like to relax in 100 degree comfort outside on a summer evening. ∎

(RIGHT) A shallow, ephemeral lake puddles the floor of Death Valley. On drying, dissolved salts will precipitate anew on the salt pan, creating geometrical patterns.
DAVID HISER/PHOTOGRAPHERS ASPEN

(BELOW) It's peak season at Sunset Campground in the Furnace Creek area of Death Valley National Park. More appealing campsites are available in the park but only in relatively small numbers. TOM BEAN

Yellow haze of late afternoon highlights a photographer on a dune crest overlooking Death Valley. RON SANFORD

Joshua Tree National Park

If improvisation is Nature's highest calling, then surely Joshua Tree National Park is a magnum opus. Two themes, each with an infinite repertoire of variations, have shaped this windswept, sun-scorched desert country.

The first theme is, naturally, a botanical one. The Joshua tree's striking presence is part and parcel of the character of the entire Mojave Desert, and the preservation of extensive Joshua tree woodlands was one of the principal reasons for establishing a national monument here in 1936.

The earliest explorers and travelers, seeking only quick passage across the desert, were hardly in the right mood to appreciate these spiny, grizzled tree-yuccas: "grotesque," "tormented," and "repulsive,"

they described them. A later group of emigrants, though, was more sanguine. In the plant's sky-directed limbs the Mormons saw the image of the prophet Joshua praying and guiding them westward to a promised land. Thus the "praying plant" became known as the Joshua tree.

Attractive or repulsive, the Joshua tree never fails as an attention-getter. There's always a fascination about the almost infinite variety of forms this strange plant can assume. In Queen and Lost Horse valleys, where Joshua trees huddle together like ragtag armies amid the boulder-studded hills, it's fun to stroll among the eerie giants and try to recognize the caricature of some familiar cartoon figure or human personality.

Warm-hued rainbows over Joshua Tree National Park capture the colors of the setting sun. Because rain-bearing clouds over the California Desert are often interspersed with clear blue patches of sky, rainfall and sunshine interact frequently, producing spectacular optical effects. JOHN DITTLI

There is an underlying order in the seemingly chaotic growth patterns of the Joshua tree. Young bucks (less than a few decades old) usually stand ramrod straight, like upturned bottle brushes. But sooner or later, one of two events—the development of a flower cluster at the terminal bud or damage to the terminal bud by insects or the elements—halts the upward growth of the trunk. Afterward, new growth takes place in the two or more new limbs that branch in random directions from just below the terminal bud. Later, the terminal buds on the

new limbs themselves are bypassed in the same way. This growth pattern, along with the tendency of some Joshua tree trunks to lean or even curl downward, results in an almost unlimited diversity of forms. The largest Joshua tree in the park, at upper Covington Flat, has forked more than one hundred times in its nearly one-thousand-year lifetime. Resembling an oversized head of broccoli, it stands thirty-six feet high and has a circumference of fourteen feet.

The second theme is a geological one. Rocks related to each other had similar origins, yet each individual rock has a unique shape—a product of circumstances during and after its formation. Throughout the monument, a younger (about one hundred million years old), lighter colored, more buoyant mass of granitic rock called monzogranite has risen to displace an ancient (nearly one billion years old), dark formation of metamorphic rock called pinto gneiss.

A hundred million years ago, the monzogranite was a molten mass, cooling and crystallizing several miles underground—a consequence of the process of subduction which was active

Shaggy limbed and spiny leaved Joshua trees take on an ethereal beauty in the warm afterglow of sunset. Joshua trees can grow to a height of more than 20 feet in a lifetime that often spans hundreds of years. WILLARD CLAY

A climber's paradise

The daily exodus begins shortly after sunrise on clear, crisp winter mornings. Soon Hidden Valley Campground in Joshua Tree National Park is half deserted. By car, mountain bike, or foot, colorfully garbed climbers fan out toward the sun-warmed formations of the Wonderland of Rocks. Outfitted with tight-fitting climbing shoes, body harness, slings, a rack of carabiners and various metal cams and wedging devices, a dangling bag of gymnast's chalk, and rope, these rock climbers might practice their art well into evening twilight.

Largely undiscovered by climbers until the late sixties, the Wonderland of Rocks has today become the nation's premier winter training ground for big-wall climbers and a year-round playground for "bouldering" devotees as well. What Joshua Tree lacks in the way of Yosemite-like scale (most climbs are only one or two rope pitches in length) is more than compensated for by the huge number of climbing routes available. The author of a popular climbing guidebook to the area (featuring nearly 1,400 already established routes on hundreds of rock exposures) notes there is still a big "untapped potential for boulder problems."

To those (usually a pair of climbers) who make the first ascent goes the honor of naming the route. Among the more interesting (and printable) names are "Mental Physics," "Quantum Jump,"

An intensely mental as well as physical game, technical rock climbing has been advanced perhaps in equal measure on the many short routes of Joshua Tree as on the big-wall climbs of Yosemite.

GALEN BOWELL

"Sole Fusion," "Thin Air," "The Taming of the Shoe," "Hyperventilation," and "Weathering Frights."

A strong sense of ethics pervades today's climbing community. Long gone is the era of chopping holds or pounding in pitons, practices that deface the rock and may irrevocably alter a route. With today's high-tech equipment, "free" climbing is now the standard. Each climber, belayed by his or her partner, climbs only on the rock itself. The rope, slings, and removable anchor devices serve as protection in the event of a fall, not as aids in the ascent.

Nevertheless, semipermanent expansion bolts are still placed on some of the new routes. Older routes have become bearded with modern-day pictographs of white chalk. If the popularity of climbing continues to increase, an even stricter set of guidelines (for example, no bolts and chalk) may yet evolve. ∎

throughout southern California at the time. As the mass crystallized, it contracted slightly, and countless joints (hairline fractures, both horizontal and vertical) developed within it. Less dense than the rock that surrounded it, this mass rose toward the earth's surface, while older layers—the overlying pinto gneiss—were eroding away.

As the monzogranite neared the surface, groundwater seeping into the joints chemically transformed some of the rock crystals into clay, a process that was especially rapid wherever the joints intersected. Eventually, large rectangular blocks with rounded corners became isolated from each other in a matrix of soft clay. Once exposed, the clay quickly washed away, leaving open cracks between the boulders.

Today, erosion continues to chip away at the monzogranite boulders exposed above the surface. The freezing and melting of water in small cracks, the impact of sand particles blown by the wind, the force of falling raindrops and sleet, and the flow of water all conspire to round the blocks still further—sometimes a single grain at a time. A more rapid process called exfoliation peels away thin layers of rock along planes of weakness. Another process is the pitting and cave formation that takes place in boulders with internal weaknesses.

Today the dark, striated pinto gneiss still covers many of the higher mountains in the park like a frosting, while the younger, light pink and tan monzogranite pokes up along the sides of these mountains. The monzogranite also thrusts high above the alluvium-filled intermountain basins and plateaus—especially in the Wonderland of Rocks area.

Wherever vertical joints predominate in the monzogranite, formations consist of columns and spires. Wherever horizontal joints predominate, the rock piles consist of stacked-pancake or loaf structures. But this pattern of regularity is obscured by the almost infinite set of outcomes for each individual boulder. Each monzogranite block has undergone a unique sequence of events and so has become one of a kind.

A more subtle but equally interesting aspect of Joshua Tree National Park is that it almost evenly straddles the two deserts of California—the Mojave and Colorado.

In the northwest and central portions of the park, the Joshua tree—a strict Mojave Desert follower—reaches the southernmost limit of its range. In the south and east, the characteristic vegetation of the Colorado Desert—smoke tree, palo verde, ironwood, ocotillo, a wide variety of cacti, and the California fan palm—reaches its northern limit. Standing within but somewhat aloof from both deserts, by virtue of collecting more rainfall, are the Little San Bernardino, Hexie, Cottonwood, Eagle, Pinto, and Coxcomb mountains, dotted with pinyon pine and juniper.

The fuzziness of the boundary between the two deserts is illustrated by the natural occurrence of two groves of fan palms well north of their usual Colorado Desert abode. The first, the Oasis of Mara (Twentynine Palms Oasis), lies next to the main visitor center just outside the sprawling town of Twentynine Palms. For nine thousand years human travelers and residents have partaken of the clear, cool waters and rested in the shade here. Over the past century, the oasis has supported several waves of prospectors, cattlemen, and health seekers. Today, a self-guiding trail winds around the grove. The surface water is gone, depleted by the pumping of nearby wells, but the palms and mesquite remain to tell of the days of Indians and pioneers.

More native palms (again well within the Mojave Desert) thrive at Fortynine Palms Oasis, hidden in a deep canyon only four miles west of Twentynine Palms. A 1.5-mile-long hiking trail, the only access, leads up and over a ridge to the isolated site.

Fan palms occur in three areas in the Cottonwood Mountains at the south end of the monument, well within the Colorado Desert. The handful of palm trees at easily reached Cottonwood Spring are not native but were planted there many years ago. Several miles east, however, two magnificent oases—Lost Palms and Munsen canyons—contain more than a hundred palms each. Both areas are accessible only by rugged trails from the west or south. Growing at unusually high elevations (at 4,500 feet near the upper end of Munsen Canyon), these palms practically rub shoulders with high-country junipers and pinyons.

The park's Colorado-Desert-dominated northeastern arm, Pinto Basin, is a typical downdropped valley bounded by faults. Here during rare flash floods, alluvium washes down from the mountain canyons and slopes onto the great bajadas that gently slope to the basin's center. The floor of the basin is building up even as faulting continues to lower its foundations and raise those of the adjoining mountains.

Today Pinto Basin is filled by a monotonous carpet of creosote bush scrub and surrounded by gaunt, gray-and-tan mountain slopes. In this bleak context, it strains credulity to realize that only two

A winter haven for thousands of shorebirds, the Salton Sea reflects the golden glow of sunset while a great egret fishes for a meal. BILL EVARTS

to four thousand years ago sparse forests covered the mountains and a sluggish stream meandered eastward along the basin's fertile floor. That permanent supply of water supported bands of Indians who left behind distinctive stone tools and arrowheads. These artifacts, indicative of a particular ancient culture referred to as "Pinto Man," are associated with many other sites throughout the California Desert.

For the tourist, Joshua Tree National Park is more than just a superb outdoor museum of natural history and anthropology. Nine campgrounds scattered throughout the park offer pleasant, though often Spartan (most lack water), accommodations. Mile-high mountain peaks and deep chasms hewn into the rock beckon both casual and serious hikers. An almost infinite variety of sheer rock faces and seamless boulders challenge rock climbers. Ten-speed bike riders tour the paved highways, while mountain-bikers bump along the dirt roads. Dozens of old mines a short distance from paved or dirt roads invite cautious exploration (without entering mine shafts). There are even special guided tours of

the Desert Queen Ranch, a well-preserved working ranch of the early and mid-twentieth century.

While over ninety percent of the park's 870 square miles is classified as wilderness, an adequate network of paved and dirt roads allows ready access to nearly every well-known point of interest. Only two paved routes traverse the heartland of the park. The first, a loop around the high northwest end, swings through Queen and Lost Horse valleys and passes near the fantastic formations of Jumbo Rocks, Hidden Valley, and the Wonderland of Rocks.

Along the second paved route, which crosses the park from northwest to southeast, the contrasts between Mojave and Colorado deserts are most graphically illustrated. Within the space of a few miles, the upper-Mojave Joshua tree forest gives way to typical Colorado Desert plants—glistening teddy-bear cholla cacti, spidery ocotillos, and puff-like smoke trees.

Of all destinations in Joshua Tree National Park, perhaps none is more rewarding than the Keys View (Salton View), reached by way of a paved spur road from Lost Horse Valley. Here, from an elevation nearly a mile high on the crest of the Little San Bernardino Mountains, a single sweeping gaze encompasses both the highest and lowest points on the southern California landscape—San Gorgonio Mountain and the Salton Sea.

Joshua Tree National Park epitomizes the "breathing spaces" so eloquently described by John C. Van Dyke and other writers nearly a century ago. Today, as yesterday, freedom rings in the clear desert air, in the seemingly boundless open spaces, and in the undisciplined expressions of both Joshua trees and rocks. Here our lives are still enriched in ways that cannot be duplicated in a world dominated by technology. ▨

The Joshua tree–yucca moth connection

A host of insects, birds, and animals are partially or entirely dependent upon the Joshua tree for food or shelter, but in only one case is this dependency a reciprocal one. The symbiotic relationship between the Joshua tree and yucca moth is very close. Neither one can survive without the other.

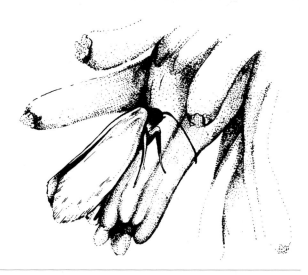

Only the small white yucca moth (*Pronuba yuccasella*) has adapted to pollinate the Joshua tree, showing interest in no other bloom.

Although young Joshua trees may sprout from the roots of a mature plant, new colonies are established only by the scattering of seeds. In many plants, pollination is accomplished by a disinterested insect intent only on collecting nectar, which, in doing so, accidentally spreads pollen. The female yucca moth, however, has evolved a special organ to deliberately transfer pollen from one Joshua tree to another. At dusk she flits about several trees, collecting the sticky pollen. After choosing a target tree, she lays her eggs in a flower's ovary and deposits enough pollen grains on the stigma to ensure fertilization and the future growth of seeds. By the time the moth larvae hatch, they find a ready supply of developing seeds to nourish them. The larvae consume only a small fraction of the seeds before they drop to the ground, leaving the rest of the seeds to be spread by the elements.

Thousands of years ago, perhaps as a result of the moth's activities, Joshua trees with sticky, easy-to-manipulate pollen were favored in the reproductive game. But their descendants lost the ability to be pollinated by other methods, such as wind dispersal or by any other insect.

How and why did the yucca moth evolve its curious behavior? No one knows. It is yet another mystery kept hostage by the mute and secretive desert. ■

Anza-Borrego Desert State Park

Juan Bautista de Anza passed this way in 1774 in search of a land route from Sonora, Mexico, to Spanish settlements along the California coast. Seventy-five years later, starting in 1849, the Gold Rush brought a steady stream of west and northbound traffic across this desert on the only all-weather overland road across the continent—the Southern Emigrant Trail. From 1858 to 1861 the famed Butterfield Overland Stage ran a mail and passenger service over the same route.

Long regarded by travelers as merely the last dry stretch short of the green and golden coastal valleys, this slice of the Colorado Desert acquired a distinction all its own in 1933 with the establishment of California's first desert state park. Named Anza-Borrego in honor of the Spanish explorer Anza and the rare desert bighorn sheep (*borrego* is the Spanish word for sheep), the park has today grown to include about 600,000 acres of varied desert terrain, much of it still as primitive as when Anza first saw it.

There are many paradoxical aspects to the park's existence. Anza-Borrego is the largest state park in California (and one of the largest in the nation, to

From a mile-high perch in Anza-Borrego's San Ysidro Mountains, a backpacker surveys a domain empty of human influence. Well over half of Anza-Borrego's 600,000 acres have been declared state wilderness. JERRY SCHAD

boot), yet many of California's residents have never heard of it. The park encompasses some of the bleakest parts of the Colorado Desert; yet hidden within at least a dozen secluded canyons, water gurgles over stone and graceful fan palms sway and shimmer in the warm breeze. Broad, monotonous plains dotted with the usual low-desert shrubs are common here, but so too are fantastic sandstone formations, boulder-frosted hills, mountain ranges topped by cool "islands" of pinyon pines, and desolate badlands shot through with twisting caverns.

The view through a sedan's windshield will do some justice to the open panoramas of Anza-Borrego, but visitors must leave the paved roads to appreciate the park's more intimate scenery. By four-wheel-drive vehicle you can meander down trench-like mudstone gorges, some flanked by cliffs over a hundred feet high, or penetrate secluded valleys tucked amid the spurs of mile-high mountains. On foot you can poke into granite-walled canyons with no tracks save those of bighorn sheep and moun-

An instant garden of sand verbena and dune primrose spreads color over the scrubby floor of Borrego Valley. LARRY ULRICH

tain lion. With a sturdy pair of hiking boots and a well-stocked pack, you can scramble up peaks offering fifty-mile-wide vistas of mountains and desert unsullied by any visible sign of civilization.

Anza-Borrego's unique geographical setting—between the snow-dusted summits of the Peninsular ranges and the bone-dry Salton Trough—contributes greatly to its special flavor. Take, for example, the remarkable variation in climates. Overnight low temperatures on the highest peaks (about 6,000 feet high) dip to near 0 degrees Fahrenheit in winter, while on the lowland flats summer daytime temperatures occasionally hit 120 degrees. Yearly rainfall, averaging a generous twenty or thirty inches in a few spots along the park's western boundary,

drops to a scant two to three inches just a few miles east.

Anza-Borrego's rainfall is biseasonal: complementing the winter showers are summertime invasions of tropical storms from Mexico. Occasionally, an erratic summer thunderstorm stalls and dumps several inches of rain over a limited area, instigating intense flash flooding and reshaping the landscape.

Geologically, the park lies in a hotbed of activity. The San Andreas Fault passes within ten miles of its northeastern corner. Dozens of smaller faults lace the park, including two of the major splinter faults of the San Andreas—the San Jacinto and Elsinore faults. Along these rifts, blocks of the earth's crust have been in constant motion over millions of years. The erosion-resistant cores of today's Santa Rosa, San Ysidro, Vallecito, Jacumba, and In-Ko-Pah mountains have risen thousands of feet while erosion has rounded their summits. These mountain ranges continue to rise and shift fitfully even in

Cannonball-shaped sandstone concretions litter a flat in the Borrego Badlands. The concretions are formed of onion-skin layers of minerals resistant to erosion.
CARR CLIFTON

the present era: park visitors were pointedly reminded of this in 1968 when a magnitude 6.4 earthquake, centered on a branch of the San Jacinto Fault, rattled across the eastern edge of the park, dislodging millions of rocks at nearby Split Mountain and smashing a vehicle.

Millions of years ago, northward extensions of the Gulf of California invaded the present Salton Trough and much of present-day Anza-Borrego Desert State Park, leaving marine sediments hundreds of feet thick. Meanwhile, the emerging Colorado River dumped loads of silt and sand near its outlet at the head of the gulf. For perhaps a million years, the lower Colorado emptied alternately into the gulf outlet or the steadily sinking Salton Trough—by then cut off from the gulf by the river delta. Each time the trough filled with water, more silt and salts from afar were deposited on its floor. The last filling episode, about two thousand years ago, created the prehistoric Lake Cahuilla, which

dried up completely only about five hundred years ago. Some rock-lined Indian fish traps and a "bathtub ring" etched along rocks west of the present Salton Sea are among the few remains of what was for a time California's biggest lake.

The titanic forces at work elevating the mountains also raised and tilted the accumulated ocean, lakebed, and riverbed sediments, exposing them to the keen knife of water erosion. The remains of these sediments, often bent or broken by further faulting, are seen today in the colorful layer-cake bluffs of Anza-Borrego's Carrizo and Borrego badlands.

The great variety of climates, geological features, soils, and topographic features throughout Anza-Borrego has spawned a remarkable diversity of plant life. In the western mountains, for example, can-

Surface water at Mountain Palm Springs serves the needs of wildlife such as coyotes, kit foxes, rodents, and birds. JEFF D. NICHOLAS

yons with year-round water support thin strips of riparian vegetation—cottonwoods, sycamores, alders, willows, fan palms, ferns, and other water-loving plants. Just outside these shady oasis-like galleries, the sunny slopes are cloaked with dense growths of cactus, agave, yucca, and drought-resistant shrubs such as brittlebush, catclaw, jojoba, and desert apricot.

In stark contrast are areas but a few miles east. Out of reach of the life-giving streams and squarely within the rain shadow of the mountains, these sandy flats and badlands are almost as austerely vegetated as the floor of Death Valley. But even here the right conditions of rainfall and sunshine can bring forth myriad wildflowers.

In March and April Anza-Borrego swarms with wildflower lovers as well as nectar-loving birds and insects. Sand verbena, desert sunflower, dune primrose, and other annuals and ephemerals carpet the sandy flats, while the rocky slopes are painted yellow by hardy brittlebush and delicate desert poppy. Spindly wands of ocotillo flush red at the tips. The waxy flowers of cholla, barrel, fishhook, hedgehog, and beavertail

A natural garden of desert agave, chuparosa, and Mojave yucca decorates a hillside in Anza-Borrego Desert State Park. The red-flowered chuparosa is a favorite of hummingbirds. LARRY ULRICH

cacti exhibit a palette of bright colors. On the margins of the badlands, white desert lilies push up through moist sand. Down on the badland washes, pink-purple desert asters stand cheerily against the gray and tan of naked sandstone and mudstone.

In terms of scenery, facilities, and sheer size, Anza-Borrego compares well with many national parks. Visitors can explore about one hundred miles of paved, scenic highway, as well as more than five hundred miles of unpaved roads. Facilities include two developed campgrounds, ten primitive camp-

Youthful fan palms at Mountain Palm Springs greet the dawn. DAVID MUENCH

grounds, and a superb visitor center near Borrego Springs in the north-central section of the park. Anza-Borrego also has a policy, unique among California state parks, of allowing open camping on nearly all lands under its jurisdiction—subject, of course, to certain rules.

Another unique feature is the resort and retirement community of Borrego Springs. This sprawling but sparsely populated island of privately owned land is completely surrounded by the park. As if to compensate for this permanent intrusion of civilization, well over half of the surrounding parkland has been designated as state wilderness. Protected from incursions by motor vehicles and visited only by a few hardy hikers, these wilderness areas serve as sanctuaries for bighorn sheep and other wildlife.

A must-see for all is Borrego Palm Canyon, with its famous groves of California fan palms. Starting at the edge of the canyon (near the park's visitor center west of Borrego Springs), an easy, 1.5-mile

Pegleg Smith and the lost gold

The most enduring, if not sober, legend of lost treasure on the California Desert revolves around one Thomas L. (Pegleg) Smith—trapper, trader, Indian fighter, horse thief, guide, and adventurer. Smith, whose leg was shattered by an Indian arrow in his youth, became (in the words of a contemporary) "the most superlative liar that ever honored California with his presence."

While moving pelts from southern Utah to the Mexican pueblo of Los Angeles in 1829 (so goes the tale), Smith picked up some curious-looking black pebbles from the top of one of three buttes located somewhere in the present-day Anza-Borrego Desert area. These pebbles, he later discovered, were really gold nuggets, their luster concealed by a dark "desert varnish."

For some years after this supposed incident, Smith pursued a living as a horse trader in various parts of the West. By 1850, however, he was back in Los Angeles spreading rumors about his long-lost gold. Offering himself as a guide, Smith organized an expedition to search for the site. After some wanderings about the desert, he abandoned his charges and showed up back in Los Angeles empty-handed. Two more futile expeditions later, his credibility presumably exhausted, he moved on to San Francisco to spend his last days trading tall tales about lost gold mines for whiskey.

Logically, Smith's fables should have departed this earth when he did in 1866. Instead the lost gold story took on a life of its own. In the ensuing decades, the supposed location of the mysterious three buttes was moved from one end of the Colorado Desert to the other, and would-be prospectors sought the treasure in everwidening circles. When interest flagged in the twenties, Harry Oliver, a Hollywood art director and founder of the "Pegleg Smith Club," spiced things up by manufacturing two hundred weatherbeaten-looking wooden legs and then salting them in various caves and mining prospects in the Anza-Borrego area.

As late as the sixties, the editors of *Desert* magazine received a sample of genuine black-coated gold nuggets from an anonymous man who claimed to have discovered the lost treasure. For years thereafter, readers of the magazine were entertained by letters directed to and answered by this mystery man, whose identity was never revealed.

Today the legend of Pegleg's lost gold lives on as heartily as ever. At the Pegleg Monument outside Borrego Springs, visitors add ten stones to a big rock pile to bring good luck in the search. Here, too, would-be Peglegs can demonstrate their yarn-spinning prowess during the annual Pegleg Liar's Contest, held on the weekend closest to April Fool's Day. Winning entries have ranged from an original thirty-four verse musical epic titled "Diablo's Gold" to a simple tale about the discovery of a rich lode of "bullsite" and "bolonium"—rare minerals that are exported to Washington, D.C., Sacramento, and other political centers. ∎

COURTESY ANZA-BORREGO DESERT NATURAL HISTORY ASSOCIATION AND MRS. HORACE SMITH

trail winds up the alluvial fan to the first grove of palms, about two hundred in number, just above the canyon mouth. During the wet months, a lively stream of water slides through the grove and tumbles

over waterfalls. More groves are secreted in the upper canyon. Elsewhere in the park more than two dozen other palm oases lie hidden away in remote coves and canyons.

Coyote Canyon—Anza's doorway from desert to mountain crest—is today the still-rugged pathway to the wildest and most beautiful scenery in the Anza-Borrego area. From the north edge of Borrego Valley, a primitive dirt road runs northwest along an intermittent stream, giving access to three jungle-like areas of willow growth along the shallow canyon bottom. Nearby are the entrances of several rugged tributary canyons, some containing waterfalls and deep pools. Coyote Canyon is closed to all public entry during the summer months to minimize contact between humans and the many desert bighorn sheep that depend on the water here.

Visitors can enjoy good views of the remainder of the park by driving the paved scenic highways out of Borrego Springs. One route, following Highway S-22 (Borrego-Salton Seaway) east toward the Salton Sea, threads a course between the base of the Santa Rosa Mountains to the north and the Borrego Badlands to the south. The Santa Rosas, stretching forty miles from Palm Springs to just east of Borrego Springs, attain a maximum elevation of 8,716 feet at Toro Peak, a familiar southern California landmark. About three hundred bighorn sheep—one of the largest herds in the state—maintain a tenuous existence along this range.

Fonts Point, four miles south of the highway by way of a sandy road, offers a startling vista of the Borrego Badlands, an intricate maze of crumbling sandstone cliffs and washes. Here, on the edge of a

(TOP LEFT) Mazes of hard-packed dry washes in the Carrizo Badlands lure intrepid joggers and hikers.
JERRY SCHAD

(LEFT) Summer cloudbursts tear at the broad face of this receding cliff in the Borrego Badlands. The promontory at the upper right was named Fonts Point, after Father Pedro Font, diarist of the second Anza expedition.
JERRY SCHAD

receding cliff, you can peer straight down into the heart of the badlands across a fantastic array of sinuous channels and razor-backed ridges carved from soft seabed deposits.

Another auto route goes south from Borrego Springs, then winds through the middle and southern sections of the park. Leaving Borrego Valley via Yaqui Pass, Highway S-3 curves sharply downward, offering a view of a classically formed bajada to the south. This is Mescal Bajada, the outwash plain of the Pinyon Mountains. Thickly covered with the gray-green daggers of desert agave ("mescal") and the foliage of creosote bush, dark green in the springtime, it can appear verdant in morning or evening light.

Jogging west on Highway 78, then south on Highway S-2—the way of the Southern Emigrant Trail and the Butterfield Stage—the route passes

Thriving amid granite boulders, an elephant tree overlooks a grove of California fan palms in the Tierra Blanca Mountains. Underlying fault cracks bring water to the surface, allowing the growth of the palms. DAVID MUENCH

through a series of stair-step valleys and leads ultimately to the lowlands of the Yuha Desert and southern Imperial Valley. The road curves around the base of the Vallecito Mountains, crowned by juniper and pinyon, and eventually drops to the hot desert floor, bristling with cactus and ocotillo.

Intriguing side roads lead east into the Carrizo Badlands. Like the Borrego Badlands to the north, these are the eroded remnants of ancient sea and lake deposits. "Reefs" thickly strewn with the fossils of shellfish and coral are common enough, but more remarkable are beds containing the fossilized bones of land creatures. Paleontologists have turned up the remains of more than a hundred nonmarine creatures such as turkey, ground sloth, horse, zebra, mastodon, camel, musk ox, rhinoceros, dire wolf, and sabertooth. Although these fossils are mostly one to two million year old, at least some of these exotic creatures were probably still inhabiting the Anza-Borrego area as recently as ten thousand years ago.

As if to mock the desolation of the Carrizo Badlands to the east, palms thrive in the

Carrizo Gorge and the impossible railroad

For a span of a little more than half a century, trains rumbled down a desert canyon once regarded by many as impossible to breach with rails.

In November 1919, after twelve years of construction difficulties and setbacks, the first through-trains of the San Diego & Arizona Railway rolled westward, freighting the agricultural wealth of the Imperial Valley over the mountains to tidewater at San Diego. Railroads elsewhere had miles of straight track, but this one turned out like 147 miles of spaghetti. The line wove through scorching desert, snow-dusted mountains, and broken foothills, even dipping south of the border into Mexico for about forty miles to take advantage of more favorable grades.

To sidestep the abrupt drip from the mountains to the desert floor, engineers had chosen a circuitous route through Carrizo Gorge, now part of Anza-Borrego Desert State Park. The rails threaded the gorge high on a narrow ledge cut into sharply curving walls of crumbling rock. Elaborate wooden trestles bridged gullies, and seventeen tunnels, ranging from 187 to 2,604 feet in length, punched through solid rock buttresses. The drop through the gorge averaged only 1.4 percent, but sharp curves necessitated slow, painstaking ascents and descents and continual oiling of wheels.

In September 1976, Tropical Storm Kathleen, the biggest chubasco to hit the California Desert in at least a century, dumped eight to ten inches of rain in as many hours on the east slope of the mountains. Large portions of Interstate 8 were washed away, half the Imperial County town of Ocotillo disappeared in a wall of water a half mile wide, and the San Diego & Arizona line was blocked or severed in at least 150 places over thirty miles. Rails hung like limp clotheslines over gullies in Carrizo Gorge.

No sooner had the necessary repairs been completed and operations resumed in 1981 than another disaster hit the railroad. A raging brush fire burned out several trestles in the gorge, again leaving the rails hanging. Despite some half-hearted attempts to repair the latest damage, it seems likely that costs, coupled with Nature's almost constant challenges, will soon permanently relegate the "impossible railroad" to the pages of history. ■

Six hundred feet long and two hundred feet high, this curved wooden trestle still stands above the desolate upper reaches of Carrizo Canyon. JERRY SCHAD

embayments and canyons carved into the hard, granitic mountains to the west. Here groundwater seeps to the surface along cracks associated with the Elsinore Fault. At Agua Caliente County Park, the water bubbles up at the same temperature as a warm bath and fills two swimming pools—one indoors and one outdoors.

Southeast from Borrego Springs via Ocotillo Wells, a narrow road runs past a stand of elephant trees, plants common to the central desert of Baja California but rare in the United States. With puffy free-form limbs, peeling yellowish bark, red sap, and purple fruit, the elephant tree is Anza-Borrego's counterpart to the grotesque Joshua trees of the Mojave Desert. Past the elephant tree area and beyond the end of the paved road lies the northern portal of the Carrizo Badlands—the awesome gash of Split Mountain, carved by flowing water cutting through a steadily rising mountain barrier. Beyond the split lies a maze of mud hills, sandstone bluffs dotted with "wind caves," and Sandstone Canyon, a two-hundred-foot-deep trench cut into multihued sandstone.

Highway S-22 west out of Borrego Springs winds up the steep slopes of the San Ysidro Mountains, offering an ever-widening view of Borrego Valley, the Santa Rosa Mountains, Salton Sea, and the distant Chocolate Mountains.

This brief narrative fails to touch upon dozens of other points of interest—some easy to reach, others not—equally worthy of attention in the Anza-Borrego area. Similarly a park brochure declines to list all the points of interest, with the comment that not all of them have been discovered yet. If this is true for a relatively small outlying sliver of California's great desert spaces, how much more lies in wait for future discovery elsewhere? ▨

The timeless desert

The desert remembers. Its rocks tell tales of volcanoes and seething cauldrons of liquid earth deep underground. Beds of soft stone harbor fossilized bones and shells of creatures from strange worlds. Ancient lakes are seen in layer-cake terraces and "bathtub" rings etched on barren hillsides. On a dry bajada, the living rim of an ancient creosote-bush ring still pledges allegiance to its ghostly parent, long since turned to dust, thirty feet inward and ten thousand years into the past.

The desert holds recent and not-so-recent memories of humans, too, such as the picturesque and mysterious leavings of prehistoric Indian cultures' wagon-wheel ruts left by emigrating pioneers a century ago; honeycombed mountains and hillsides strewn with rusting mining equipment; immense, semipermanent geoglyphs gouged by military tank maneuvers; the geometric designs of cities, towns, and vast agricultural and public works enterprises (visible as dominant features of the desert on satellite photographs); and, not insignificantly, the patterned prints of off-road vehicles that rolled over stretches of hard desert crust yesterday—or a decade ago.

These memories we have inherited today, and some of them—even modern ones—are as indelible as any on earth. Perhaps the most important question we can ask about the desert now is: What other memories, locked into the desert landscape shall we bequeath our descendants?

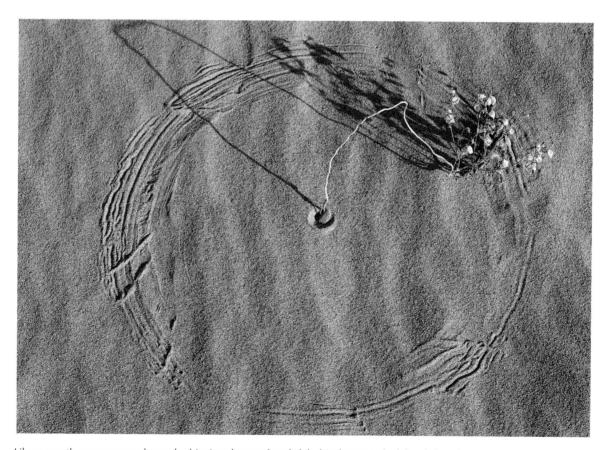

Like a weather vane gone berserk, this tiny desert plant left behind a record of the shifting breezes. DAVID MUENCH

The California deserts of two centuries ago were some of the purest kinds of wilderness on earth—avoided by all but the toughest forms of life, including most humans. Even a hundred years later, the desert's severe climate and lack of easily exploitable resources kept it from being well integrated into the economic mainstream of the continent.

A century ago, aside from the prospectors and stockmen who tried to wrest a living from it, no settler in his right mind thought of living in the desert by choice. Summers were insufferable. Other than minerals and sparse forage for livestock, there was little to exploit in the desert. No great forest or water resources dependable enough to support agriculture or cities or big industries drew the interest of developers. But railroads, highways, and, to a significant extent, air-conditioning changed all that.

The desert challenged us with the elements—heat, cold, dryness, wind—and physical obstacles like mountains and sandy wastes. It also lured us with promises of material gain and bountiful living. With the help of twentieth-century technology, we responded by molding the desert into our own contemporary image. Row crops and minerals, resorts, towns and highways, aerospace industries, and military complexes became the symbols of human domination.

But now we are faced with a new challenge. The desert is already burdened enough with memories stamped on it by human influence. Although we have it in our power to permanently alter the desert on a more colossal scale than ever before, we must deliberately choose to put the brakes on unbridled exploitation.

Only recently have we come to recognize some of the hidden, long-term consequences of meddling with the desert environment. Even so benign a practice as irrigated agriculture is subject to serious difficulties: without adequate drainage, salts contained both in irrigation water and in desert soils build up in the root zones of crops, restricting yields and ren-

Open-pit borax mine pocks the surface of Death Valley National Park. TOM BEAN/DVM

dering some areas useless for further agriculture. "Tiling," the installation of perforated pipes under the fields to flush away the saline irrigation water, is a workable solution, but this adds to the salt burden of areas downstream.

The tapping of "fossil water" under the desert is another promising but short-term form of exploitation. Water drawn from desert aquifers is not usually a renewable resource. Once it is depleted, more than a thousand years of scant rainfall and percolation may be required to replace it.

Even though we have long possessed a technology capable of chewing off half a desert mountain and then sifting, cooking, and digesting its

contents, only recently has it become common practice to weigh the potential commercial benefit of a mining project against its negative environmental consequences. How much pollution of the air, groundwater, and soil can the desert sustain?

Only recently, too, have millions of people come to appreciate the desert for its natural values—the

En-masse motorcycle racing in the California Desert is permitted along certain corridors by special BLM permit. Hundreds of cyclists gather annually to make the 152-mile Barstow-to-Las Vegas trek, which roughly follows the route of Interstate 15.
CRAIG AURNESS/WEST LIGHT

The emerging metropolis of Palm Springs spreads across the desert from the base of the San Jacinto Mountains. The population of the greater Palm Springs area exceeds 100,000. GALEN ROWELL

solitude and tranquility it affords, the wonderful scenery, the richness of its plant and animal life. But these values are fragile.

It is said that in the human perception of solitude and tranquility, a hundred acres of open desert equal that of just one acre of dense forest. What, then, are the consequences of putting in a single road across a formerly roadless stretch? How much will its visual ambience be compromised? If the road is open to all comers, how often and how far will the roar and whine of dirt bikes and all-terrain vehicles push back the silence?

The real California Desert—the unimproved desert—is still the largest reservoir of undisturbed open space in California. We must set aside and jealously guard blocks of desert land where humans are

but temporary visitors, and where primitive means of transportation are the norm. In other areas we must try to salvage some of the original character of the desert while simultaneously allowing a multiplicity of uses. The ethics of protection must become standard practice among desert users.

Today California's deserts help support the "good life." Their mineral, energy, plant, and food resources help to maintain our high standard of material wealth. With careful stewardship, we can maintain both these values and others of a nonmaterial nature. We can bequeath to our descendants the same timeless desert we enjoy today—the crystalline skies, silence, and unlimited space that lighten our spirits and purify our souls. ▣

Names on the desert

There's an old anecdote about a disgruntled miner who couldn't help complaining about "working the graveyard shift at the Coffin Mine, located in the Tombstone Mountains of the Funeral Range overlooking Death Valley." The story is probably apocryphal, but it illustrates how the harsh and bleak desert landscapes of California have spawned their fair share of interesting and often grim-sounding place names.

Colorful place names serve as a mirror by which we may view, in an oblique way, the lives of the early explorers, gold seekers, stockmen, farmers, government surveyors, and the assorted riffraff and oddball characters who frequented or settled the California desert area.

Unfortunately, relatively few of the original Indian names for California desert sites are in use today. A few contemporary names, however, were derived from the names of tribes or the dialects spoken by those tribes: *Panamint Mountains, Piute* also *Paiute, Pahute Range, Mojave* (also *Mohave*) *Desert, Shoshone* (a town), *Chemehuevi Mountains, Lake Cahuilla.* Other Indian names are descriptive: *Coso* ("fire") *Mountains, Ubehebe* ("big basket in the rock") *Crater, Hanaupah* ("bear water") *Canyon, Inyo* b("dwelling place of a great spirit") *County, Jacumba* ("hut by the water") *Mountains, Tuba* ("pinyon nuts") *Canyon.*

Spanish names are more common, especially in the Colorado Desert—though even here they are not as abundant as along the California coast. Examples of desert place names of Spanish origin are *Amargosa* ("bitter") *River, Cerro Gordo* ("fat hill") *Mine, Pinto* ("painted") *Basin, El Centro* (the town at "the center" of the Imperial Valley), *Borrego* ("sheep") *Valley, Agua Caliente* ("hot water") *Springs, Arroyo Salado* ("salty creek"), *Dos Cabezas* ("two heads") *Spring,* and *Vallecito* ("little valley") *Moun-*

tains. Many Spanish place names are associated with saints (*San* or *Santa*) as in *Santa Rosa Mountains.*

About ninety percent of all place names in the California desert are of English-language origin. Some refer to the local vegetation, wildlife, and geography. Others are historical or personal. Still others are purely descriptive, often in a quirky sort of way.

Fruit growers and speculators, for example, contributed names like *Pearland, Pearblossom,* and *Apple Valley* to areas of the Antelope Valley and Mojave Desert they hoped to develop for agriculture and housing.

Minerals and mining activity are reflected in such names as *Gold Mountain, Gold Shot Mine, Copper Basin, Leadfield, Antimony Spring, Carbonate Mine, Chloride Cliff, Boron, Saline Valley,* and *Soda Lake.* The names of many of the mines themselves mirror the aspirations and sometimes-wry humor of the miners: *Black Magic, New Deal, Green Hornet, Mystery, Rainy Day, Golden Egg, Rockefeller,* and *Revenue. Skidoo,* a mining camp near Death Valley, took its name from a popular expression of the early century—"twenty-three skidoo"—because the water pipe built to serve it was twenty-three miles long. On the edge of the Anza-Borrego Desert, a mine intended to be named the "Gold Reef" ended up, by virtue of someone's poor penmanship, being officially recorded as the *Cold Beef Mine.*

The implication of grimness is inherent in many desert place names, yet the origin of some of the following names had little or nothing to do with grim qualities: *Starvation Canyon, Dry Bone Canyon, Horse Bones Canyon, Poverty Hills* (no one could find gold here), *Dead Mountains, Jail Canyon, Breakneck Canyon, Chaos Ridge* (named by a geologist for its broken and irregular character), *Furnace Creek* (named for an abandoned lead furnace here, not for the ferocious heat), *Funeral Range, Last Chance Range, Lost-man Spring, Groaner Spring, Headache Springs, Arsenic Spring, Tough Nut Spring, Poison Spring, Tin Can Spring* (not a spring at all, but a place where water was cached), *Pluto's Salt Pools, Suicide Pass, Dead Man Pass, Badwater, Hells Gate,* and *Hellhole Canyon* (a hell of a place to remove a stray cow).

Even the devil himself was not exempt from commemoration. Examples are *Devils Canyon, Devils Playground, Devils Golf Course, Arroyo Seco del Diablo* ("dry creek of the devil"), and *Devils Elbow.*

Desert plants are recognized in such names as *Grapevine Canyon, Mahogany Flat, Wildrose Canyon, Smoke Tree Wash, Tule Canyon, Palm Canyon, Twentynine Palms, Palm Springs, Pinyon Mountains, Iris Wash, Palo Verde Valley, Ocotillo Wells, Cottonwood Spring, Juniper Flat, Willow Hole, Mesquite Mountains, Carrizo* ("cane") *Canyon, Cactus Mountain,* and *Yucca Valley.*

Wildlife names include *Jackrabbit Hill, Lynx Cat Mountain, Coyote Canyon, Sheep Canyon, Goat Spring, Quail Spring, Owlshead Mountains, Eagle Mountains, Bird Spring, Jackass Spring, Porcupine Tank, Antelope Valley, Burro Spring, Bat Caves Butte, Tarantula Wash, Chuckwalla Mountains, Serpents Mesa,* and *Buzzard's Peak.*

Some duplication of place names is inevitable and understandable for an area as large as the California desert, but in some cases the duplication has reached absurd levels. There are, for example, at least half a dozen canyons that go by the name *Rattlesnake Canyon.* There are five separate *Granite Mountain(s);* of these, three are located in San Bernardino County—all within a circle only a hundred miles across.

Here and there a bit of regular nomenclature surfaces on the California desert. More than a century ago, the locating engineer for the Santa Fe Railroad across the Mojave desert named the stations along the route in alphabetical order (a common practice at that time): *Amboy, Bristol, Cadiz, Danby, Edson, Fenner, Goffs, Homer, Ibis,* and *Java.* Some of these later became noted stops along the National Trails Highway—Route 66—and Ibis became the short-lived Camp Ibis used for troop training during World War II.

Some desert names—ironic, clever, or simply outlandish—are mysterious, too: Are *Soggy Dry Lake* and *Drinkwater Dry Lake* really dry? Was the remote railroad station called *Styx* really named after the river of the Underworld, or was it originally intended to be "Sticks"? Was *Sneakeye Spring* named after a thief or a spy? Did hungry miners enjoy a hearty meal at *Fried Liver Wash,* or was it named because of the flat, desert-varnished rocks that line it? Was *Dirty Sox Warm Springs* named after a sulfurous odor or because miners used it as a natural Laundromat? Are the nudists who frequent *Oh-My-God Hot Spring* shocking, or is it just the scalding temperature of the water? Did wild bacchanals ever occur at *Satyr's Rockpile?* Was *Zzyzx* (mineral springs) intended to be merely a tongue-twister, or simply the last entry in the phone book? Was it a Californian or a Baja Californian who dreamed up the names for the twin border towns of *Calexico,* California, and *Mexicali,* Mexico?

Finally there are names that dispel all speculation about their origin: *Unnamed Wash, Canyon Sin Nombre* ("canyon without a name"), and *Quien Sabe* ("who knows?") *Point.* ▨

A favorite of photographers, these dunes cover the floor of Death Valley near Stovepipe Wells.
FRED HIRSCHMANN

Places to visit

Major desert parks and recreation areas:

Anza-Borrego Desert State Park
P.O. Box 299
Borrego Springs, CA 92004
(619) 767-5311

California Desert Conservation Area
(BLM)
Main Office
6221 Box Springs Blvd.
Riverside, CA 92507
(909) 697-5200
Barstow Resource Area
(619) 255-8700
El Centro Resource Area
(619) 337-4400
Needles Resource Area
(619) 326-3896
Palm Springs Resource Area
(619) 251-4800
Ridgecrest Resource Area
(619) 384-5400

Death Valley National Park
Death Valley, CA 92328
(619) 367-7511

Joshua Tree National Park
74485 National Monument Drive
Twentynine Palms, CA 92277
(619) 367-7511

Mojave National Preserve
Office
222 East Main, Suite 202
Barstow, CA 92311
(619) 255-8800
Information Center
P.O. Box 241
Baker, CA 92309
(619) 733-4040

Visitor centers, museums, smaller parks, and preserves:

Antelope Valley California Poppy
Reserve
4555 West Avenue G
Lancaster, CA 93534
(805) 724-1180

Antelope Valley Indian Museum
c/o 1051 West Avenue M, Suite 201
Lancaster, CA 93534
(805) 942-0662

Big Morongo Canyon Preserve
P.O. Box 780
Morongo Valley, CA 92256
(619) 363-7190

California Desert Information Center
831 Barstow Road
Barstow, CA 92311
(619) 255-8760

Hole-in-the-Wall Visitor Center
Black Canyon Road
Mojave National Preserve
(619) 928-2572

Interagency Visitor Center
Drawer R
Lone Pine, CA 93545
(619) 876-6222

Living Desert Reserve
47-900 Portola Avenue
Palm Desert, CA 92260
(619) 346-5694

Malki Museum
Morongo Indian Reservation
Banning, CA 92220
(909) 849-7289

Palm Springs Desert Museum
101 Museum Drive
Palm Springs, CA 92262
(619) 325-7186

Picacho State Recreation Area
P.O. Box 1207
Winterhaven, CA 92283
(619) 339-1360

Providence Mountains State
Recreation Area
P.O. Box 1
Essex, CA 92332
(805) 942-0662

Red Rock Canyon State Park
P.O. Box 26
Cantil, CA 93519
(805) 942-0662

Saddleback Butte State Park
17102 Avenue J East
Lancaster, CA 93534
(805) 942-0662

Salton Sea State Recreation Area
P.O. Box 3166
North Shore, CA 92254
(619) 393-3052

Santa Rosa Mountains National
Scenic Area Visitor Center
51-500 Highway 74
Palm Desert, CA 92260
(619) 862-9984

"Coyote melon," actually an inedible gourd, grows amid the cholla cactus gardens of Joshua Tree National Park.
LARRY ULRICH

About the author

Jerry Schad, a fifth-generation Californian, has worked as a freelance writer and photographer for over twenty years, specializing in science, travel, and the outdoors. His contributions have appeared in more than twenty regional and national publications. He also teaches astronomy and physical science at San Diego Mesa College. *California Deserts*, the seventh of his eleven books, is the outgrowth of his long love affair with the desert, sparked in 1972 by a springtime visit to the palm groves at Anza-Borrego Desert State Park. Enthralled as ever with the desert, he continues to spend much of his time exploring the wild spaces from Death Valley to Baja California.

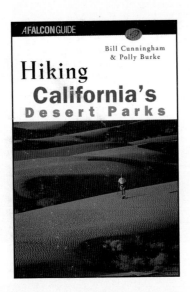